Discovering the Secrets of Business Success in Ancient Biblical Wisdom

ORLA KELLY
PUBLISHING

Val Mullally

For contact details see https://valmullally.com

ISBN 978-1-912328-55-0 (paperback edition)

Published by Orla Kelly Publishers, Cork, Ireland

Orla Kelly Publishing
27 Kilbrody, Mount Oval
Rochestown, Cork
Ireland

Dedicated to my husband

you are the wind beneath my wings

About the Author

Val Mullally is an Authopreneur, international Keynote Speaker, Online Course Provider, accredited Life and Relational Skills Coach, and Supervisor.

https://valmullally.com

Her purpose is to help people to:

- think more clearly
- connect more compassionately
- behave more response-ably
- and live more joyfully.

Resources by Val Mullally

Online courses in Relational Skills

https://koemba.thinkific.com

Online BizWisdom Masterclass Series - the exclusive support group for your business success: https://valmullally.com

Follow her on social media:

LinkedIn:https://linkedin.com/in/valmullally

Facebook:

https://facebook.com/BusinessSuccessFromAncientWisdom

Pinterest: https://pinterest.ie/valmullally

Twitter: @valmullally

Contact Val on author@valmullally.com

Please use this hashtag when you mention this book on social media: #BizWisdomBook

In Praise of "Discovering the Secrets of Business Success in Ancient Biblical Wisdom"

I have been in business for many years and have to say that I have never thought of looking to the Bible for insights on business success, until I read Val Mullally's book, *Discovering the Secrets of Business Success in Ancient Biblical Wisdom*.

This book, based on insights from ancient spiritual texts, can afford us clear, powerful and empowering principles and skills which are timeless, if we embrace them with an open mind and heart.

The book integrates Val Mullally's intensive study of biblical wisdom with her personal and professional experiences and offers us both inspiration and practical guidance to finding workable solutions to the modern-day business challenges we face. She shows us how practical biblical wisdom can help us genuinely connect with ourselves and others to deepen business relationships, learn how to better serve the needs of our customers and at the same time improve productivity.

She articulates a strong case for utilising biblical wisdom to inform our practice of consciousness in a world of polarity and complexity. It is a masterful integration of biblical insights and practical examples with many invitations to reflect on and integrate new skills into our own business context. Val delivers simple, doable, ground-breaking approaches, based on traditional spiritual wisdom that can help you develop your performance ability, increase productivity and serve your clients with quality products and services, with dignity and respect.

Elizabeth Garry Brosnan
EGB Soulpreneurs
www.egbsoulpreneurs.ie

Val shares her story of seeking the truth and how she finds the Proverbs not only has the answers but the book of Proverbs is the answer.

A book that was written thousands of years ago and yet more relevant today than it was then. It is no surprise that Solomon was the richest man in the Bible. I have found that many successful business people are people of great faith and live by biblical principles.

Val has brought wisdom to the forefront of every reader's mind, reminding us of the huge benefits from seeking wisdom.

This is a book you will want to buy for your friends and colleagues because it's not just some day you need wisdom, you need wisdom every day!

Amanda Delaney
We Can and We Will – Ireland
www.amandadelaney.ie

Discovering the Secrets of Business Success in Ancient Biblical Wisdom hits the nail on the head, especially for those entering a leading position in the business world. It diminishes the doubts and encourages positive thinking.

This book gives guidance and support to believe in your vision and to accomplish the journey to a successful business.

Sophia Elisabeth la Cour

This book is so well-written and a must for business owners and for anyone setting out on a new business venture.

Maeve Murray
Postpartum Doula

Having accepted Val's request to proof-read her latest offering, *Discovering the Secrets of Business Success in Ancient Biblical Wisdom*, I could not have imagined how very much I would love reading it! Proverbs have always been amongst my favourite biblical texts and the seeming simplicity of Val's explorations belie the depths of her insight and sagacity.

I loved being taken on this initial journey of challenge and self-discovery, and I look forward to spending deeper times with Val's book, plumbing for wisdom to apply in both my personal and business life.

Claire Latinis Forde
LLB, Mediator

You can follow new updates and discussion about this book by using the hashtag #BizWisdomBook

For more information, visit: https://valmullally.com

Foreword

In this era of rapid technological development, we have a tendency to over-value the new.

We can't wait for the next update. We assume the latest version is better than the previous one. Older models are discarded, assumed to be relatively worthless.

This relentless pursuit of the "next thing" has influenced our thinking too. We seek the freshest ideas, the new angle, the up-to-date analysis.

As children, we have a tendency to believe that our parents' generation just don't get it. They don't understand the modern world. They can't see things like we can. The old rules no longer apply.

But when it comes to wisdom, the cumulative gathering of intelligence (and capability) on how to live in this world, then this novelty-seeking philosophy begins to lose value. It turns out that the active pursuit of the new, the constant seeking of the latest, puts us on a path that eventually brings us to a destination where we finally understand what those who preceded us were on about.

In this creative and refreshing book, Val Mullally reminds us that what we perceive to be the latest, cutting edge perspectives on how to thrive in the modern business world are not as novel as we might believe. She shows us that any activity involving human beings will invariably be improved by tapping into a source of timeless wisdom about how to show up fully as a person in whatever it is we do.

Just like the laws of physics underpin the evolution of the universe we live in, so too do a set of timeless truths about the human condition. In our excitement to discover something novel about ourselves and the world we live in, we often forget that someone just like us may have already made such progress in the same spirit of wonder and adventure, even if they lived millennia before us.

You'll find yourself reacting with delight and surprise when you see some of the gems of wisdom that Val has mined from her study of biblical scriptures. Even better, your enjoyment of this book does not depend on you holding any particular faith or religious worldview. The wisdom tends towards the universal and the adventure that Val brings us on, in the spirit of role model Indiana Jones, is open to new discoveries.

In my own professional practice over many years, I've worked with thousands of people to help them expand their working wisdom. One of the essential elements of the work I do in the executive coaching field is to create a comfortable space for clients to reflect and gain clarity on their professional lives.

To adapt a definition suggested by Stephen Fry, wisdom is ultimately about the ability to cope, with whatever life throws at us. And having read over five hundred books in the areas of business, performance and psychology, I can assure you that Val's work here is a fresh addition to the literature.

Val's skilful design of this book presents us with a rich opportunity for reflection by giving us multiple opportunities to pause and explore the meaning within some of the well-crafted proverbs, as well as holding up a mirror to our present activities and approaches. Her encouragement to actively engage through journalling is great advice and I would also suggest taking your time in your journey through the multi-faceted lessons that lie ahead of you in this book.

Val Mullally, just like you and I, is on a journey of adventure. None of us is surrounded by certainty but by bringing courage to her exploration of timeless wisdom and having the open curiosity to find useful answers no matter where the source, she has done us all a great favour.

It's up to the rest of us now to follow, with pen in hand and both eyes and heart open, ready to discover the guidance that can illuminate our way.

Aodan Enright
Executive Coach | Founder and Facilitator of Smarter Egg: helping you develop your working wisdom

Contents

About the Author..v

In Praise of "Discovering the Secrets of Business Success in Ancient
Biblical Wisdom"..vi

Foreword ix

Introduction: This Book is For You.. xv

SECTION A: How It All Began xvii

Chapter 1: Setting Out on the Journey to Successful Business 1

Chapter 2: Mastering a Mindset of Wealth - a First Step....................3

Chapter 3: The Wake-Up Call 5

SECTION B: Seeing the Big Picture 7

Chapter 4: Deciphering Ancient Clues 9

Chapter 5: Why Wisdom is the Keystone 13

Chapter 6: Knowing the "Why" of Your Business 17

Chapter 7: Why Wisdom Matters 21

Chapter 8: Going for Gold 23

**SECTION C: Studying the Treasure Map for the Business of
Your Dreams** 25

Chapter 9: Information Overload - Time Wasters 27

Chapter 10: Priorities and Productivity 31

Chapter 11: Know the Key Metrics of Your Business 35

Chapter 12: Laser Focus - With Love 39

Chapter 13: Finding Your Support Network...43

Chapter 14: Other Eyes on the Business 45

Chapter 15: Observe Nature 49

Chapter 16: Going for Gold 53

SECTION D: Igniting Your Business Success **55**

Chapter 17: Craft Your Elevator Pitch 57

Chapter 18: Ancient Tips for Digital Marketing Success 61

Chapter 19: The Seduction of Get Rich Quick 69

Chapter 20: Why Generosity Matters 75

Chapter 21: Leading Your Team 79

Chapter 22: Ethics in Business - the Foundation of Success...................87

Chapter 23: Going for Gold...95

SECTION E: When Business Doesn't Go Smoothly **97**

Chapter 24: When Things Are Beyond Your Control 99

Chapter 25: Who Do You Hang Out With? 101

Chapter 26: The Balancing Act 105

Chapter 27: Laziness and Procrastination 111

Chapter 28: How to Be a Transformer...117

Chapter 29: Persevering in the Face of Failure 121

Chapter 30: Why Self-Discipline is Pivotal for Success.......................125

Chapter 31: The Wisdom of Good Work Habits 129

Chapter 32: Going for Gold...133

SECTION F: Your Inner Journey as Successful Business Person 135

Chapter 33: Beliefs - a Different Perspective 137

Chapter 34: When the Going Gets Tough................................141

Chapter 35: Dethrone Ego 145

Chapter 36: Ego's Shadow - False Humility 153

Chapter 37: Can Our Gut-Feeling Lead to Wisdom? 155

Chapter 38: When a Leader Compromises Their Integrity...............159

Chapter 39: Seek Knowledge and Understanding.................163

Chapter 40: Going for Gold 165

SECTION G: The Awesome Treasure of IQ, EQ and More..................167

Chapter 41: The Essential Keys to Relationship Success.................169

Chapter 42: Talking Wisely..175

Chapter 43: Listening Wisely 183

Chapter 44: Developing Super-Power Listening Skills.................189

Chapter 45: Break Free from Anxiety, Procrastination and Overwhelm 197

Chapter 46: How to Ensure Anger Does Not Crack the Whip 201

Chapter 47: From Conflict to Connection 205

Chapter 48: Intuition - Tuning in to Inner Knowing................213

Chapter 49: Going for Gold 219

SECTION H: Be the Difference That Makes the Difference 221

Chapter 50: The Power of Healthy Relationships................223

Chapter 51: Why Boundaries Matter 229

Chapter 52: The Amazing Power of Discretion................233

Chapter 53: Staking Out the Territory of Social Justice 237

Chapter 54: Stand for Social Justice 243

Chapter 55: Champion Those Who Can't Speak for Themselves 249

Chapter 56: Light the Torch of Leadership 253

Chapter 57: Wield Transformative Power 257

Chapter 58: Going for Gold 263

SECTION I: The Epic Adventure of Business Success **265**

Chapter 59: Seek Wisdom - the Source of All...267

Chapter 60: The Pitfalls of Ignoring Wisdom 271

Chapter 61: Treasures Beyond Belief 275

Chapter 62: The Discovery 281

Appendix 1: How I Unearthed Treasure in Ancient Biblical Texts **283**

Appendix 2: Tips for Exploring Ancient Biblical Texts...**285**

Help Val to Help Other Entrepreneurs...**289**

Recommended Resources for Business Success **291**

Bibliography...**293**

Other Books by Val Mullally **296**

Acknowledgements **297**

Endnotes **299**

Introduction

This Book is for You

This book is for you if:

- you want to change your passion into profitability and make a difference in the world,

- you want to align yourself with the successful people who put in the consistent effort to create success,

- you are serious about considering these time-proven principles of Wisdom. Only then will you discover their transformational power for your business and your life.

This book presumes a belief in the Divine Power of the God portrayed in the Bible, who desires our well-being. At the very least it asks your willingness to temporarily "park" your disbelief to consider these messages from ancient Wisdom.

You will probably find it helpful to read the first section of the book to understand the context of the book. Feel free to read the chapters in whatever order attracts you, although I recommend reading all the chapters within a section in their sequence, because, in that way, you are likely to gain the most benefit, as the natural progression of thought unfolds.

I invite you to use a journal to record your responses to the questions in the "Time to Reflect" sections at the end of most chapters; this will help you gain the most from this guide.

If you're serious about achieving your unique purpose in life, let's step into this business adventure together.

The biggest adventure is to live the life of your dreams.

Oprah Winfrey

SECTION A

How It All Began

Chapter 1

Setting Out on the Journey to Successful Business

A change was underfoot: the shift towards success began slowly. Like the imperceptible change of tide, no difference was at first discernible, but there was a memorable moment.

On a trip to Dublin I met up with my good friend and colleague Rebecca Mahon. Over the years she has been generous in sharing her business insights. We hadn't seen each other for months so I imagined a time of relaxed "girl chat"; but it wasn't long till she asked how my business was going. Soon her focused questions had us deep in conversation.

"Why do you give so much of yourself to helping me with my business?" I asked.

She looked squarely at me, shrugged and continued with her line of thought.

It was an earnest question I'd asked. A business mentor would charge a significant fee for the insights she was sharing: this was a gift of friendship. We dug into my business, turning over the clods of day-to-day grind, and scrutinising what we unearthed. All too soon it was time to end the session. As I picked up my handbag, Rebecca suddenly said,

"About the question you asked: I help you because I'm curious how long it will take you to figure this out. You have so much to give to the world, you should be a millionaire!"

Those words will always stay with me. Somebody believed in me and my potential beyond what I could dream. I know that for me, **touching a million lives is mega more important than making a million euro.** Yet my challenge is to create a successful business, because this makes it possible to create the resources that can help others. Affluence, to me, means that riches flow through a person to serve others. I had to discover what is needed to create a successful business.

Capitalism – which, in its purest form is entrepreneurism even amongst the poorest of the poor, does work; but those who make money from it should put back in society, not just sit on it as if they are hatching eggs.

Richard Branson[1]

Chapter 2

Mastering a Mindset of Wealth - a First Step

A little later that day, I had time to browse in a bookshop. I headed straight for the business section. I needed to find the answers to my questions about how to create wealth. Within minutes, I found Jen Sincero's book *You Are a Badass at Making Money: Master the Mindset of Wealth*. I liked the book's layout, with questions to encourage personal reflection. *This would be a good purchase!*

In the following days, as I worked through the exercises in Sincero's book, I reflected on my childhood money story. I grew up in a secure home with a stay-at-home mother and a civil-servant father. Ours was a home where there was enough to eat and the privilege of having parents who loved each other, but with four children there were few luxuries.

My father was a civil servant. I pondered this term as I journalled. A servant is one who does the bidding of another - not following one's own dream. My dad enjoyed his career but he followed his dreams in his off-work time.

This was an era that was a far cry from today's millennials - when a girl was expected to be a secretary, an air hostess, a hairdresser, a bank teller or a teacher. I wanted to be an artist but my dad insisted I needed to get a "real job" so I could earn a living. I did what was expected. I enjoyed my teaching career, but now, in a different chapter of my life, I'm stepping into the adventure of a lifetime. My quest is to become a successful authorpreneur. I am discovering how to turn my passion into a profitable business.

I reflected on the childhood money story I'd absorbed. I unearthed a couple of unhelpful messages from my early life, which needed to be rooted out. These phrases popped out in my memory:

"They're filthy rich …"

"We're stony broke."

As I journalled, those phrases intrigued me.

"Filthy" - disgusting, polluting, repugnant, disease carrying

All these years I had carried a subconscious message that money was repugnant.

And what about being "stony broke"?

Stony ground - rock hard, unyielding, no growth, barren, sheer hard work for little return. I had imbibed a mindset of stony broke, and this was something I needed to change! I needed a rich and fertile "soil" to create and grow resources that would nurture and sustain others. How could I develop a healthy relationship with money if these childhood messages were what I believed! If I wanted to create a successful business, I needed a different, healthier attitude towards wealth. What would it take to master a mindset of wealth?

> *What's money for anyway? It makes things happen.*
> **Richard Branson**[2]

At this point I could not have imagined the secrets I was about to uncover that would lead me to the business success so far beyond what I had dreamed.

Chapter 3
The Wake-Up Call

I'd love to tell you it all turned around in one day. It would be great to tell you that after my "aha" moment everything immediately turned around and I was making thousands in a couple of weeks. No. That didn't happen. Things got tougher. My influence was increasing but my affluence wasn't. It was costing me more to produce resources than I was gaining from them. I needed a better business model - one that worked!

Then I came across a small Kindle book by Ben Settle: *Christian Business Secrets - how to use ancient laws to build a thriving godly business in today's cut-throat marketplace.* And here's the nugget from Settle's book, in his interview with Terry Dean, which sowed the seed of writing this book:

Don't seek Wealth – seek Wisdom.[3]

The lights came on for me. I knew this wasn't just another chapter in a book I was reading. Here was a blockbusting, life-changing, adventure – with the promise of as much intrigue and exhilaration as an Indiana Jones movie. Would I have the courage to step into it?

Where would I find Wisdom? There are plenty of knowledge books about how to create business success. But I was on a different search; I was seeking something much deeper and richer. How was I going to unearth Wisdom? I discovered an ancient treasure map that you might even have in your home.

Where is this treasure map? It's buried in the very heart of an ancient text and it's called the book of Proverbs. If you want to find it, you'll locate it just after midway in the Bible.

What is the story behind this ancient scripture? Over two thousand years ago a new king succeeded his father. Solomon had big shoes to fill and, I imagine, he felt daunted by the enormity of the task of governing the Israelite people. As the ruler of a kingdom, he believed his life's purpose was to lead his people well, and he asked God for Wisdom in order to do this.[4] Solomon was a magistrate[5]- making decisions in situations of legal contest. He was also the key writer of these ancient wisdom sayings in Proverbs. I had read these scriptures before, but now a new thought struck me:

Solomon must have been a businessman! How would he have managed his huge wealth if he didn't understand business? Yes, he probably had a team of astute accountants and financial advisers, but I figured he had insight into what is needed to create successful business. And King Solomon became one of the wealthiest men in the whole world - ever!

And the Bible records that **Solomon didn't seek wealth. He chose Wisdom.**[6] **And wealth followed as a natural outcome.** It made sense to me that a person would not be likely to accrue wealth unless they knew how to handle business. So, here's what I decided: I'd study the book of Proverbs from a business point of view and see what age-old success secrets I could uncover. I was going to need an archaeologist's mindset to decipher the message of these ancient texts.

I'm not an archaeologist. I'm not a qualified theologian or an historian. I'm a regular gal with a vision of resourcing parents to create calmer, happier family life. I'm an entrepreneur with a big dream. And this message struck me: Don't seek wealth – seek Wisdom. Join me on this adventure to discover the treasures of Wisdom and unearth riches you and I have never dreamed of. Together we'll find the amazing secrets that Wisdom unlocks to creating successful business.

Solomon has rolled out the treasure map on the table. Are you willing to leave the comfort of life as you've known it and set out on what could prove to be the greatest adventure of your life?

Money is not the goal. Money is the fuel.

Simon Sinek

Seeing the Big Picture

Chapter 4
Deciphering Ancient Clues

Before I begin to share with you what was revealed to me, let's first look at how neuroscience, the study of the structure and function of the brain, can help us unlock the secrets of Proverbs, hidden in plain sight for over two thousand years. Understanding how our brains work will help us to see why the imagery of Proverbs can be so powerful in shifting our thinking to see a new paradigm of business success.

The thing is, the book of Proverbs is not a "to do" list. Rather, it is poetry, using imagery that unfolds when we reflect on the verses. These images are often referred to as metaphors in literature and psychology because they contain much deeper meaning than is apparent at first glance. What we now know is that metaphor engages a different part of our brain functioning than that used to consider a set of rules. Imagery captures the attention of the right hemisphere of the brain - the creative part of our thinking - including our ability to see patterns in what can first seem unrelated thoughts. **Imagery expands our awareness and lateral thinking of other possible aspects and of nuances in the text.** When we use right-brain functioning, as well as left-brain, we are in an exciting place, where learning sticks and transformations happen.

Here's an easy way to remember the dominance of the brain hemispheres, and why both aspects matter.

Left Brain = Logic

The epitome of left-hemisphere thinking is Star Trek's Mr Spock, the resolutely logical human-Vulcan, who is intelligent yet unable to tune in to his emotions or those of other people.

Right Brain = Creativity

The right hemisphere processes emotions and finds meaning in the metaphor - it's the part of the brain that "unpacks" the message within the image. The right hemisphere plays with Proverbs to decipher their deeper meaning, or to see wider perspectives.

Engaging both left and right hemispheres ignites our intuition, our imagination and our empathy, allowing us to see and feel another person's experience. We gain new insights and discover unexpected treasures.

When you first read the Proverbs, it is easy to skim the surface with only the left-brain engaged – a "Yes. I know that!" reaction. But, like visiting an art gallery or listening to a piece of beautiful music, one needs to slow down to notice how seemingly random aspects are skilfully intertwined. When we pause and reflect, we notice how some aspects are emphasised through repetition; we notice the attention to detail in particular aspects. We observe the depths of the composition and new angles we hadn't noticed before. We become aware how juxtapositions, light and shadow amplify the richness and the message of the artist's work.

When we bring both hemispheres of our brain on board, we notice these subtleties and can delve into deeper levels of understanding. This matters because **reading Proverbs without absorbing their message will not create transformation.** We need to explore the images and notice patterns if we want to unlock their treasures.

> *... let the wise listen and add to their learning,*
> *and let the discerning get guidance—*
> *for understanding proverbs and parables,*
> *the sayings and riddles of the wise.*

Proverbs 1:5,6

A riddle is a cleverly worded phrase that requires ingenuity to ascertain its meaning. The imagery used in these ancient texts also makes the principles of Wisdom far more memorable, which means, if we are in "whole-brain-engaged" mode, they will influence our thinking and actions long after we have first read them.

May I remind you to use your journal at the end of each chapter to pause and reflect on what new insights might be unfolding for you. This matters if you want to integrate the wisdom of this book into your life and business.

The human species thinks in metaphors and learns through stories.
Mary Catherine Bateson

Time to reflect:

What piece of literature, music or art, or natural object catches your attention today?

As you pause to reflect on it, what thoughts and feelings does it evoke?

In what ways might greater awareness and "whole brain engaged" improve your business?

Let's discover insights within the book of Proverbs that will guide you to create perennial business success. Here's how to **transform your passion into profitability, live your life fully and make a difference in the world.**

Chapter 5
Why Wisdom is the Keystone

If Wisdom is the keystone we're seeking, then we're headed in a different direction to the average Jo Soap Entrepreneur. We will discover mysterious and exciting territory that only a few have explored. We will explore the landscape of a transformed world, where the consumer-focus of most businesses is a dinosaur. We will discover the value of creating a model of business that is sustainable for the future. Let's together create businesses that inspire hope and possibility.

Our journey needs to begin with asking ourselves, "Why does my business matter?" In his book *Start With Why: How Great Leaders Inspire Everyone to Take Action*, Simon Sinek proposes the foundation for achieving anything is knowing *why* it matters - understanding the purpose. Join me and discover what King Solomon, an incredible leader and mighty businessman, shares about the secrets of success.

Why Does Wisdom Matter?

If you're the regular hard-working, multi-tasking entrepreneur, you've got to be convinced a book is going to prove valuable to you before you'd take time from all the other demands on your life, to commit to read it. So, let's look at the opening words of a book that has remained favourite reading for two millennia.

Within a few verses of the first chapter, Solomon draws us in to the book of Proverbs[7] with a graphic description of how life falls apart without Wisdom. He warns us:

~ don't take advantage of others nor cause pain;

~ don't hang out with people who will lead you into trouble;

~ don't put in huge effort without gain.

He declares that if we ignore Wisdom:

~ we won't be able to call on Wisdom when disaster sweeps over us like a whirlwind, when calamity,

~ distress and trouble overwhelm;

~ we will reap the consequences of our unwise choices;

~ our *complacency* will destroy us.

Complacency is defined as "a feeling of smug or uncritical satisfaction with oneself or one's achievements that prevents one from trying harder".[8] We might think we're doing fine, but when the storms of life hit, we won't have what's needed to weather them if we haven't "tried harder" – if we haven't done the work to gain Wisdom.

King Solomon builds the case for why Wisdom matters. He lists the benefits of choosing Wisdom:

~ knowledge and understanding

~ victory (*I imagine that's what every entrepreneur wants!*)

~ ability to share knowledge and understanding

~ protection from evil

~ discernment in the life decisions you need to make

~ upright living.[9]

What it Takes to Gain Wisdom

Solomon makes it clear that Wisdom is not a "pick and choose" option. It's a way of being. Wisdom calls us to a life-long commitment:

Let love and faithfulness never leave you,
bind them around your neck,
write them on the tablet of your heart.

Proverbs 3:3

When Solomon talks about a "tablet" he's not referring to medication nor to an iPad! People didn't have the everyday writing implements that we now take for granted, so important instructions were carved into stone. To emphasise that these teachings are to be indelibly imprinted upon our lives, in this day and age, when we don't write on tablets of stone, he might have said:

"Tattoo love and faithfulness on your heart."

Wisdom is not something you peel on and off. Wisdom is for life.

In Solomon's "elevator pitch", he has told us what we have to gain, what is needed and the consequences of ignoring Wisdom. He has also told us where seeking Wisdom will lead:

~ prosperity[10]

~ clarity regarding the way ahead[11]

~ health and vigour[12]

~ longevity[13]

~ honour[14]

~ peace.[15]

Isn't this what every business person desires: for business to go well and for life to go well.

Any fool can know. The point is to understand.

Albert Einstein

King Solomon explains what Wisdom is and why it matters![16] We'll explore how to create a powerful elevator pitch once our journey is underway.

Ancient, intuitive wisdom is what our frantic, high-tech global village needs.

Richard Branson

Time to reflect:

What are you willing to give to gain Wisdom?

Which of these qualities most strongly beckon to you?

- prosperity
- clarity regarding the way ahead
- health and vigour
- longevity
- honour
- peace

What would these mean to your life and business?

We've looked at why Wisdom matters - now let's look at the "why" of your particular business.

Chapter 6

Knowing the "Why" of Your Business

In the book of Proverbs, we have the map that can lead us to Wisdom. Let's scrutinise it carefully before we set out. If this is going to transform our business beyond our wildest imaginations, we need to start out with a clear plan and we need to know where we are headed.

Solomon immediately sets out his purpose in writing Proverbs:

for gaining wisdom and discipline ...

Proverbs 1:2a

When I began to search the book of Proverbs I felt as though I was entering an archaeological dig. I needed to proceed slowly and carefully so I didn't miss vital clues. I decided I would write out by hand whatever verses or thoughts struck me. Why did I do this? Initially, at a logical level, I couldn't have answered that. It was intuitive. I normally work on my laptop but I sensed I needed to slow my process. It made me consider everyday English words instead of automatically presuming I knew their definition.

for receiving instruction in prudent behaviour ...

Proverbs 1:3

Prudent - what does that actually mean? I know it sort of means "wise" - but why this particular word?

This book is not a study of Greek or Hebrew, I'm just trying to decipher the English words!

"Prudent - acting with or showing care and thought for the future."[17]

Wow - isn't that a clear business principle. It emphasises taking action *now* to create the future we desire; a future not only for our benefit but our legacy for future generations. More about building business for the future when we get to the chapter about Kresse and Elvis!

I have a clear sense of the "Why" of my business.

I support parents and leaders in business and community to:

~ think more clearly

~ connect more compassionately

~ behave more response-ably

~ and live more joyfully.

The bottom line is, why does our business matter? What is the purpose of our business? Are we hell-bent on "What's In It For Me?" schemes? Or **is your business providing quality service or resources, to create a better world, social justice, health, peace, connection and understanding?** If you want to create business that is much more than a money-making machine, then this book is your path to discovering the secrets of Wisdom. **Our businesses can become more than "business as usual" – they can be vocations.**[18]

Vocation, even in the most humble of circumstances, is a summons to what is divine.
Richard Rohr[19]

Time to reflect:

What is the big "Why?" of your business and your life?

Take time to write it out in your journal. You need a clear vision of your destination if you want to get there.

Now that we've looked at the "Why" of our business, what is a key image in Proverbs that will remind us of our true destiny?

Chapter 7

Why Wisdom Matters

We've chatted about the "Why" of our business. Solomon gives a clear "why" in Proverbs chapter three – the heading: "Wisdom Bestows Well-Being".[20]

Solomon explains:

> *[Wisdom] is a tree of life to those who take hold of her;*
> *those who hold her fast will be blessed.*

Proverbs 3:18

As I read "tree of life" I thought of the beautiful tree of life design often depicted in Irish jewellery - roots deep in the soil, as the branches stretch upwards and outwards.

Before you read further, you might choose to pause and reflect on what the image of "tree of life" evokes for you. You might wish to download a blank copy of the tree of life image: https://valmullally.com. You could choose to write in key qualities of Wisdom on the roots, trunk and branches as you reflect on these chapters.

> *The one who gets wisdom loves life;*

Proverbs 19:8a

The "tree of life" is one of the earliest symbols relating to the Divine. It suggests that ours is more than an earthly journey.

~ It's about being grounded - being firmly rooted in that which really matters.

~ It's about reaching out - giving nurture, shelter and sustenance to others.

~ And it's about leaving a legacy - something that is going to survive to bless future generations.

Know also that wisdom is like honey for you;
If you find it, there is a future hope for you,
and your hope will not be cut off.

Proverbs 24:14

A long life may not be good enough, but a good life is long enough.

Benjamin Franklin

Time to reflect:

What is evoked within you when you reflect on the image of the tree of life?

In what ways does this image invite you to fulfil your God-given destiny?

Let's recap our journey so far, as I share with you one of my favourite movie characters.

Chapter 8

Going for Gold

As we have been talking about deciphering ancient clues, let me introduce you to one of my movie favourites. If you don't already know him, Indiana Jones is the legendary hero in the film series created by George Lucas and directed by Steven Spielberg (from 1981 onwards) including *Raiders of the Lost Ark* and *Kingdom of The Crystal Skull*.

We meet Indiana as a very ordinary professor of archaeology. Soon we are swept along on his mission through remote jungle or parched desert in search of long-lost treasure. He dodges poison arrows, collapsing edifices and huge rolling boulders that have annihilated other would-be adventurers. He outsmarts dangerous enemies, rescues damsels and evades gruesome death. He survives! He finds the way through treacherous territory to victory!

You can't think about Indiana Jones without thinking of his iconic fedora, confident stature, self-deprecating wry smile, gentle humour and quick wit. He's a very human human - he doesn't rely on hugely bulging biceps, James Bond gadgets or super-powers. He's a down-to-earth person we can identify with. He believes he can do it - and he does! Indiana succeeds where others fail because his eyes are wide open for the cryptic clues - and he knows how to decipher them.

Like Indiana, we can learn to dodge the traps, elude the dangers, outwit the enemies and discover the ancient treasure, *when we know what to look out for.* Proverbs can guide us through the snares and lead us to success. We need to be as alert and observant as Indiana, with whole-brain engaged to solve the enigmatic clues written by King Solomon and his other writers. Proverbs is an ancient map that will lead to indescribable riches if we solve the puzzles. Just as Indiana's ability to read the cryptic clues saves him from danger and leads him to the treasure, we can learn to decipher Proverbs, so we can bypass the potential disasters and achieve our goal.

Let's reflect on our journey in this section. (More about Indiana later!)

What we can gain from Proverbs:

~ understanding why Wisdom is the keystone for business success

~ discernment in our life and work decisions

~ the ability to do work that matters to leave a lasting legacy.

Wisdom leads us to creating business that is so much more than a money-making machine. The true gold of success isn't about accruing wealth; it's about fully living a life that counts and leaves a legacy. When we seek Wisdom we are on a life-time adventure of discovery.

> *… look for it as for silver,*
> *and search for it as for hidden treasure,*
>
> **Proverbs 2:4**

Finding Wisdom is not easy. It's like mining silver - it takes commitment, perseverance and hard work. And you'll need to keep focused on the long-term vision: gaining Wisdom! This is not a quick fix. This is a life-long commitment. It's a way of being. And it will be worth it.

In the next section we'll begin unfolding this age-old plan to discover Wisdom's key principles for success. What can this treasure map reveal about creating the business of your dreams?

Studying the Treasure Map for the Business of Your Dreams

Chapter 9

Information Overload - Time Wasters

Indiana packs his bags, and the adventure begins.

For us as entrepreneurs it isn't always that easy or immediate to figure out how to start.

What do I need?

What information matters most?

How do I know what I need to know?

These are challenges for every entrepreneur. There's so much to take in.

> *... knowledge comes easily to the discerning.*
>
> **Proverbs 14:6b**

Discern means to "perceive by the sight or some other sense or by the intellect".[21] When we are discerning, we are clear about what we choose to give our time to. Like any other ability, the more it's practised the stronger it becomes. It gives us the power to notice what's working; what's not. What is helpful; and what's not. It is closely linked to observation and intuition, which we'll get to in a later chapter. **If you observe astutely, slow down and listen to your gut, you will sense what needs attention; you'll discern the time-wasters.**[22] You will sharpen your perception skills.

Discernment is part of the Wisdom package. The natural knock-on effect when you seek Wisdom is that your ability to judge well will improve. And better discernment means better business.

Discernment has a close cousin that is also valuable to the entrepreneur - prudence.

… the prudent give thought to their steps.

Proverbs 14:15b

The one resource we most need to give thought to is our time. It's the one resource we cannot replenish. When it's gone, it's gone. We might gain more money or more resources but we will never gain more time. Are we spending our time wisely?

Prudence is a fountain of life to the prudent,

Proverbs 16:22a

We can fall into the trap of being so busy working in the business that we forget to work on the business. Wisdom develops as we take time to reflect upon our work and to plan - ideally a check-in each day and a block of time each week and month-end to step back and notice what's working, what's not and what's needed.

The discerning heart seeks knowledge,
but the mouth of a fool feeds on folly.

Proverbs 15:14

Everything we say yes to requires that we say no to something else.

Derek Draper

Time to reflect:

What daily, weekly monthly, quarterly and annual habits have you developed to assess your business?

What other habits and systems to you need to develop to discern what's needed in your business?

So, discernment matters, but how does that pan out in our day-to-day decision making?

Chapter 10
Priorities and Productivity

Setting out into foreign territory can be confusing, disorienting and sometimes nerve-wracking. It takes courage. Worry can be the constant companion of the entrepreneur.

Will this work out ok? What's around the corner? Prioritising means we will figure out what is most important, so we can take corrective steps in time to avert disaster. In the next chapter, we'll look at the importance of our business metrics; watching the dashboard to assess what's working, what's not and what's needed. If we are consistently alert, we'll spot potential dangers and prioritise to take precautionary action that will enable us to skilfully manoeuvre through the challenges we face.

> *The prudent see danger and take refuge,*
> *but the simple keep going and pay the penalty.*
>
> Proverbs 22:3

It's easy to be busy - but are we busy with the right things in the right way at the right time? Have we prioritised what matters most?

We can't effectively prioritise unless we have determined what our priorities are.

> *Put your outdoor work in order*
> *And get your fields ready;*
> *after that, build your house.*
>
> Proverbs 24:27

Every farmer knows that the season for productivity is not a constant. In other words, use your time and resources to do the essentials first while the conditions are good to do them.

> *I went past the fields of a sluggard,*
> *past the vineyard of someone who has no sense;*
> *thorns had come up everywhere,*
> *the ground was covered with weeds,*
> *and the stone wall was in ruins.*

Proverbs 24:30

As I typed this verse, my Macbook auto-corrected "slacker" for "sluggard"!

Years ago, my husband and I bought a smallholding that had been neglected for a long time. The field was so filled with weeds we couldn't even use a tractor to clear it. The vents of the radiator became blocked with the weed seeds within a few yards, overheating the engine and making it a near-impossible task. Keeping the field weed-free hadn't been a priority and the ground was useless until that was achieved. You're probably not planting a field, or repairing stone walls, but what preparatory work, weeding or repair of work boundaries need your attention? My email box jumps to mind. What needs weeding out? What limits do I need to ensure that this technology is a useful tool and not a rampant briar choking my productivity?[23]

> *He who gathers crops in summer is a prudent son,*
> *but he who sleeps during harvest is a disgraceful son.*

Proverbs 10:5

Prioritising well means taking time to work on the business - to step back, see the big picture and reflect on what's needed. It's not only what we choose to do but when we do it. **Without effective prioritisation we add to our workload and stress.**

> *… a rod is for the back of one who has no sense.*

Proverbs 10:13b

PeopleSpeak: He's making a rod for his own back.

With the personal discipline of planning our work and working our plan we create the business we desire.

> *Whoever heeds discipline shows the way to life,*
>
> **Proverbs 10:17a**

In his era and culture, Solomon saw the pattern of what's needed to create abundance.

> *When the hay is removed and new growth appears*
> *and the grass from the hills is gathered in,*
> *the lambs will provide you with clothing,*
> *and the goats with the price of a field.*
> *You will have plenty of goats' milk to feed your family*
> *and to nourish your female servants.*
>
> **Proverbs 27:25-27**

Everything has its season. There will be a good return when we put in consistent work at the right time.

> *Only once you give yourself the permission to stop trying to do it all,*
> *to stop saying yes to everyone, can you make your highest contribution towards the things*
> *that really matter.*
>
> **Greg McKeown**[24]

Time to reflect:

What do you see as your life and business priorities?

Looking at your diary and your financial record, what are your actual priorities?

What are the biggest issues in your business that need your attention now - the important as well as the urgent?

What do-able step will you take today to ensure you are prioritising what matters most?

How and where can you discover the systems you need to improve your prioritisation skills?

So, figuring out our priorities is one thing, but how do we discern what's working?

Chapter 11

Know the Key Metrics of Your Business

Sometimes we are in such a rush to reach the treasure of success we aren't checking our "compass" to see if we are on track. Like Indiana flying the plane through uncharted territory, how will we know all is going well, or that something needs attention unless we are aware of the information on the dials? Each business is different, but – just as the pilot checks the altimeter, temperature and fuel gauges – there are key metrics that every business person needs to consistently monitor to ensure all is going well, or to assess where attention is needed.

If we lose our way, we waste time, energy and resources as we try to realign. When we're monitoring our progress, we can take action when needed to correct our course to ensure we arrive at our destination.

> *Be sure you know the condition of your flocks,*
> *give careful attention to your herds;*
> *for riches do not endure for ever,*
> *and a crown is not secure for all generations.*
>
> **Proverbs 27:23,24**

These verses make me think of the careful monitoring for bovine TB I had seen in Ireland. Without early intervention to arrest any outbreak of disease, a farmer's whole herd could be destroyed. In business, as in farming, health and well-being has to be vigilantly assessed to ensure ongoing success.

We need to know our plan and regularly check we are heading in the right direction if we want to get there.

Desire without knowledge is not good —
how much more will hasty feet miss the way!

Proverbs 19:2

We need to read our key metrics and realign as we go. And if we are looking for funding or business partners, those key metrics are essential to get financial support. And that makes sense because when we consistently check our metrics we won't be wandering around - *wondering* whether we are doing the right thing! Wisdom is the True North that guides us.

The righteousness of the blameless
makes their paths straight,

Proverbs 11:5a

As I read this Proverb, I notice it doesn't say, "God will make their paths straight." It says our own right-living will smooth the way. This will be a natural consequence when we make wise choices.

We need to stand back, read the key metrics and look at the big picture:

What's working?

What's not?

What needs adjusting?

It's not enough to work *in* our business; we need to work *on* our business.[25]

What gets measured gets managed.

Peter Drucker

Time to reflect:

What are the three key metrics of your business that you need to consistently track?

How, where and when are you recording those?

What or who is helping you to check on your business health?

How are you using this information to work on your business?

Reading the key metrics is essential, but how do we turn our knowledge into powerful outcomes that move the dial to business success?

Chapter 12

Laser Focus - With Love

Indiana Jones is alert. He doesn't miss the tripwires that could spell disaster. He reads the clues that guide him to his goal. He keeps his attention entirely on the task at hand. He doesn't try to multi-task, as so many of us do in our busy lives. And what we now know from brain science is we don't multi-task; we switch from one job to another. And each switch causes a temporary loss of focus. What this means for the wise business-person is the need to focus on one job at a time. Remove and turn off all other distractions.

This is still an area that challenges me. I forget to switch off my email before I start writing and the notification of an incoming message will grab my attention. I don't open the mail, but the alert has drawn me away from my focus on my writing. Research shows it takes over 23 minutes to fully return your focus to a task after an interruption.[26]

I have read so many articles on why laser focus matters, I knew it is seen as a key business principle, but would I unearth it in Proverbs? *Aha- there it is!* Proverbs 4:25 says to let your eyes look straight ahead - "fix your gaze directly before you." If you are looking straight ahead you are not letting yourself be distracted by what is on the margins.

The word "gaze" intrigues me. It has a different feel to the clinical sound of "laser focus". The verse doesn't say, "stare directly before you"! The word "gaze" evokes looking at something steadily and intently, yet there is an implication of something soft, loving and embracing of beauty. We gaze at our beloved, an exquisite flower or sunset. Whilst the word "stare" indicates a certain vacancy, "gaze" implies being fully present. Being mindful.

So, we could say: **Give your complete, present and loving attention to what you are doing.** This thought intrigues me. I can see how that will benefit my writing, but giving my complete, mindful present and loving attention to an email or working with the finances? That's a challenging thought! I know I lose my passion when I try to adopt a clinical "laser focus"—to be motivated and inspired I need to gaze on my projects with love!

So how do we apply mindful attention to the big picture of our business?

A discerning person keeps wisdom in view,
but a fool's eyes wander to the ends of the earth.

Proverbs 17:24

Some people are always looking for the "New Thing", starting this, then that - without giving time for the seeds of a new venture to germinate and take root. In contrast, Wisdom is prudent and recognises some things take time to take root. We need to keep our soft gaze attentive to our project. Wisdom seeks the long-term potential. The discerning person is one who carefully evaluates, and keeps the goal in sight. And this leads to consistency. One of the reasons unseasoned entrepreneurs keep hopping from one new idea to another is because of the seeming lack of growth in a project.

In his book *Scaling Lean*, Ash Maurya indicates that the trend of the finances of most successful businesses is rather like a hockey stick placed on its side along the ground, with the hook facing upwards.[27] The financial graph indicates a long straight, almost horizontal line, until eventually there is a sudden and strong upward rise. **We may become discouraged and be tempted to give up on a project when perhaps the upward sweep to success was just before us.**

When we are watching our key metrics with a mindset of "laser focus – with love" we will have a sense of where we are and where we are headed.

The road to success is always under construction.

Arnold Palmer

Time to reflect:

What happens when you choose to "gaze directly" at the task you love to do, giving it your complete, fully present and loving attention?

What happens when you take a "laser focus - with love" approach to a task that you normal dislike or hurry through?

What impact might "laser focus - with love" have upon the big picture and long-term success of your business?

Knowing the key metrics of our work, having a clear business plan, and knowing our priorities can help us to determine where we need to fix our gaze. But what do we do when we don't know what to do?

Chapter 13
Finding Your Support Network

Nobody does a solo act. Not even Indiana Jones. His keen knowledge of archaeology gives him insights to what's needed when he's deep into unknown and dangerous territory. How does he know what's needed? He studied, his father mentored him and he has other allies along the way.

> *… victory is won through many advisers.*
>
> **Proverbs 24:6b**

We need to recognise that **the journey to success is not a solo path.** We need trustworthy advisers. Ask yourself, "Who are the authors, bloggers, podcasters, webinar presenters or course presenters who can help me fill in the knowledge gaps?" I also find it helpful to work with a business adviser, a mentor or a coach.

And likewise, consider joining at least one networking group where you feel you are on the same page as the other group members. It's not only about joining a group, it's about joining the group that's right for your business. This morning was our "Biz Rocking Gals" group - a monthly online meeting, which is one of my greatest time investments. This small group has developed a strong sense of mutual trust and support. Sometimes a shared insight sparks a sense of *Why didn't I think of that!* Sometimes our advisers spot the obvious we can't see. I'm blessed by the generosity and wisdom of my peers in this group. It's a win-win! We all need other eyes on the business.

Perfume and incense bring joy to the heart,
and the pleasantness of a friend
springs from their heartfelt advice.

Proverbs 27:9

Imagine how much easier it would be to succeed in life if you were constantly expecting
the world to support you and bring you opportunity.

Jack Canfield

Time to reflect:

Who are the people you turn to for sound business advice?

What has been a transformational business learning you have gained? Who was your advisor?

What business question is uppermost in your mind now? Who could you ask for advice?

Networking is a great way to get your business questions answered, but what can you do when you don't know that you don't know?

Chapter 14

Other Eyes on the Business

We all have blind spots. Even Indiana sometimes ends up in trouble because there's something he has overlooked. He misses the quick glance that passes between two people, that signals to the viewer that there's a devious plan unfolding.

In a similar way, there are things we don't know, or things we can't see, or sometimes our vision becomes cloudy or distorted. **We need to have a group of people whose wisdom and expertise we trust to help us look at our business - what we're doing, how we're doing and why we're doing.**

> *... do not trust your own cleverness.*
>
> **Proverbs 23:4b**

One of the good things about having "other eyes on the business" is it forces us to be accountable - to ourselves as well as others. You can't be accountable without recording and assessing the key metrics. And other experienced eyes can often help to read and interpret those metrics.

> *The prudent see danger and take refuge,*
> *but the simple keep going and pay the penalty.*
>
> **Proverbs 22:3**

Interestingly, Proverbs 27:12 has almost identical wording. Phrases are repeated to emphasise their importance. The prudent - those who show care and thought for the future - notice the trends and take action to protect their business before calamity strikes. One of the benefits of other eyes on the business is that those people can ask questions and make observations that help you ascertain what is working and what is not. Often, it's putting time, resources and energy into what's not working that takes the shine off our business - like the chemical reaction that tarnishes silver.

Remove the dross from the silver,
and a silversmith can produce a vessel;

Proverbs 25:4

You can't make something beautiful, useful, valuable and lasting unless you get rid of the dross - the things that are not adding to the quality of the product. And often it takes "other eyes" to see what's needed. Seeking wise advice is repeated in several Proverbs:

The wise in heart accepts commands.

Proverbs 10:8a

… whoever heeds correction shows prudence.

Proverbs 15:5b

Mockers resent correction,
so they avoid the wise.

Proverbs 15:12

… whoever ignores correction leads others astray.

Proverbs 10:17b

For lack of guidance a nation falls,
but victory is won through many advisers.

Proverbs 11:14

A rebuke impresses a discerning person …

Proverbs 17:10a

At the same time, this is not about heeding the advice of every person we meet.

One who has unreliable friends soon comes to ruin,
but there is a friend who sticks closer than a brother.

Proverbs 18:24

Of course, we need to test the wisdom of advice - and having "other eyes" on the business isn't going to have impact unless we put into effect the advice we are given.

As "other eyes" help us to become the wise leaders we desire to be, so we, in turn, mentor others. It's often in supporting others that we clarify and challenge our own skills and ways of working.

As iron sharpens iron,
so one person sharpens another.

Proverbs 27:17

Accountability requires making space to reflect, evaluate and plan ahead.
Ultimately it's about doing the right thing.

Derek Draper

Would you love to have Val Mullally's "wise eyes" on your business? Val is an accredited coach and offers an exclusive online masterclass series to those who are serious about changing their passion into profitability, and making a difference in the world. Click on this link to discover more: https://valmullally.com

Time to reflect:

Who are the "other eyes" whose business advice you trust?

Do your "other eyes" give insight into all the different aspects of your business, or is there someone else you need to ask onto your support team?

How and when do you meet up with your "other eyes"?

How do you ensure this time with advisors is an investment (for them as well as for you)?

Other business people can be a great source of support, but have you considered one of the greatest sources of Wisdom that is right before your eyes?

Chapter 15
Observe Nature

Let's take a moment to think about a real-life adventurer from a much earlier era than Indiana. Imagine Christopher Columbus' voyage into total uncharted seas; a venture so risky it could have meant death for the entire crew. Columbus had no guarantees or back-up options. There were no radio devices; no rescue aircraft.

During the whole of his discovery journey, he altered his course only twice to find the "New Land". After sailing for twenty-eight days - nearly a month! - he changed direction. Why did he change course? Because he noticed a great number of birds flying from North to Southwest. Within days they spotted land. [28]This saved the expedition at least a day's travelling and perhaps prevented the crew's mutiny. Christopher Columbus looked to Nature for guidance, and so did Solomon.

I applied my heart to what I observed
and learned a lesson from what I saw:

Proverbs 24:32

Solomon observed Nature. Besides being a magistrate and businessman, he was a naturalist.

He spoke about plant life, from the cedar of Lebanon to the hyssop
that grows out of walls.
He also spoke about animals and birds, reptiles and fish.

1 Kings 4:33

Solomon looked for Wisdom in the everyday. He mined the ordinary. In Proverbs 6:6, he even invites us to learn from the ant! Ants don't work for the sake of working; they work to achieve a particular purpose. They bring home the bacon - sometimes literally! They cooperate with one another to achieve their goal. They clear their path of obstructions. They work to attain their objective and to secure a future for their community.

Here's an observation I noted that has hugely impacted my business mindset:

Many streams of revenue create a river.

As an author, this is about having my books available on different outlets, creating digital, paperback and audio versions, advertising my availability as a coach and motivational speaker and creating online courses from my material.

Nature also demonstrates there are cyclical patterns. There are times to prepare the ground, times to sow, times to harvest and times for the ground to lie fallow. There are dry periods and wintry days, and there are times of abundance. The season is not "wrong" - it just is - and we need to look for the beauty and blessings within it.

Observing nature can bring unexpected insights.

… to search out a matter is the glory of kings.
Proverbs 25:2b

I love the intricate beauty of nature and its attention to design —the perfect symmetry in the butterfly's wings, the amazing spiral within a snail's shell. There is joy in the detail. **Taking time to reflect on the environment around us can sometimes give fresh insights into our business.** When we have an open loving gaze, we might sometimes notice messages that could transform our work, not only in nature but also in unexpected places: a slogan, a newspaper clipping, the lyrics of a song.

Look deep into nature, and then you will understand everything better.

Albert Einstein

Time to reflect:

What have you observed in Nature and your surrounds?

How might this observation be transferred to your business acumen?

Where might you seek inspiration?

Let's take a look at Indiana as we reflect on the key thoughts in this section.

Chapter 16
Going for Gold

When you first meet Indiana, you may think he's a nerdy professor. As the camera zooms in on him at the front of the lecture room, it pans across his desk. You notice the globe of the earth, and primitive artefacts. This man is much more than he seems at first glance. The bell rings for the end of the session and before we know, we are whisked out of the lecture room and into a world of mystery and adventure.

To set out on the entrepreneurial adventure we need to study the treasure map for the business of our dreams. If you were on a real-life adventure with Indiana, you'd want to be able to compare your map with the realities around you to figure out if you are on track - to check you are where you are meant to be. You would want to know what lies before you and where you need to be heading. Taking time to record and study the key metrics of your organisation are the essential reality pointers you need to check against the map of your business. The key metrics alert you if you are heading in the wrong direction. Ignore them at your peril.

And, like Indiana, we need to keep focused on the task at hand. **We need to be fully present to what is before us, even when the heat is on. Especially when the heat is on!** It's about being mindful within our business; what I term "laser focus - with love". Even if doing the financial books isn't our greatest love, we can learn to give them our mindful attention, when we recognise this is our regular check-in on the treasure map of our own business. We need to laser focus with love to ensure we are on course.

Indiana Jones might seem a lone ranger, but he didn't gain his essential knowledge of archaeology without mentors. At times, he checks in with his father. Older eyes can be wiser eyes. In business we need a support network. We need mentors to help us see what we are missing. We've also looked at the value of observing and learning from nature. In fact, we can observe and learn in whatever setting we find ourselves, when we slow down to notice. A book title, a slogan, a reflection of the sky on glass panes. What speaks to you today?

And we've looked at discernment, which gives us the power to observe what's working, and what's not. Clear judgment helps us to step back and notice what builds a successful business.

Apply your heart to instruction
and your ears to words of knowledge.

Proverbs 23:12

I note this proverb does not say, "Apply your head to knowledge." Throughout literature, the heart is used to denote love and passion. I wonder if Solomon is conveying a love of learning. Knowledge comes more easily to the discerning because they take the time to figure out their priorities. They know where to put their attention and why it matters.

With Indiana's keen eye, it's time to look at how to ignite your business success.

Igniting Your Business Success

Chapter 17

Craft Your Elevator Pitch

If you want a business that successfully sells its products or services, **you need a clear call of what you're selling and for whom it is.** If you have trained in marketing you are familiar with the term "elevator pitch".

If you were in an elevator at the same time as someone else, by the time you reach the upper floor, would you have been able to describe your business in a way that excites a potential customer that this is something they need? Solomon wouldn't have had an elevator but he knew how to make his pitch! He is 100% certain about his "Why?", "What?" and "Who is this for?"

Why?

> *for gaining wisdom and instruction;*
> *for understanding words of insight;*

Proverbs 1:2

Solomon is clear about the purpose of what he is presenting.

What?

> *for receiving instruction in prudent behaviour,*
> *doing what is right and just and fair;*

Proverbs 1:3

Who is this for?

... for giving prudence to those who are simple,
knowledge and discretion to the young –
let the wise listen and add to their learning,
and let the discerning get guidance –
for understanding proverbs and parables,
the sayings and riddles of the wise.

Proverbs 1:4-6

In these verses above, Solomon refers to the simple, the young, the wise and the discerning. Biblica[29] explains that "simple" may also be translated as "gullible".

Here Solomon explains what can be achieved from "buying" this offer. He clarifies who is his target audience – who will benefit from this product. He has clearly set out his stall of what he is offering, its purpose, and who it is for.

Who is this not for?

Solomon also includes for whom this is not!

... fools despise wisdom and instruction.

Proverbs 1:7b

What is a "fool"? The Hebrew word refers to someone who is "morally deficient".[30] Wisdom is not for the morally deficient.

Clearly defining your audience also means identifying for whom your work is not. A product that is made to try to meet everyone's needs will satisfy no-one. As Holiday says,

"The best art divides the audience."[31]

Crafting Your Elevator Pitch Clarifies Your Thinking

What many don't realise is that writing your elevator pitch is as much a tool for your benefit as it is for your customers. It pushes you to think clearly about what your business provides, who is it for, and what purpose is it serving. If you can't succinctly describe your business in a few sentences, you need to spend more time at the drawing board.

Look again at my elevator pitch:

I support parents and leaders in business and community to:

~ think more clearly

~ connect more compassionately

~ behave more response-ably

~ and live more joyfully.

It states who is my target market, what it sets out to achieve and, in the last line, it declares my "why" – to live more joyfully.

Now it's your turn to craft and examine your elevator pitch. In crafting it, you are not trying to reach everybody. **The job of your elevator pitch is to be a clarion call for those who would want what you have to offer.** It's about letting your particular audience know that you understand their desire, or the problem they are facing and that you have the solution, or are able to alleviate their stress. And it's about expressing this with heartfelt energy because people will connect with your passion.

Think left and think right and think low and think high.
Oh, the thinks you can think up if only you try!

Dr Seuss

Time to reflect:

Why does your business matter? What is its purpose?

What specifically do you intend your business to achieve?

Who is your business for?

Now figure out how you would say this in a two-minute elevator ride!

In the next chapter we'll look at sharing the message of your business with your tribe. Obviously digital marketing wasn't available in Solomon's day, but you'll be surprised at how much wise advice he has on this topic.

Chapter 18

Ancient Tips for Digital Marketing Success

When I when I started researching these ancient biblical texts, I never thought that I would find digital marketing gems. Was I in for a big surprise!

1. Don't ask a dishonest price.

Don't trick your customer to think they are getting more value than they are really getting.

The LORD detests dishonest scales,
but accurate weights find favour with him.

Proverbs 11:1

It's an old trick to weight the scales so the customer gets less value for their money than they believe they are receiving. We might not have physical scales but do we give our customers genuine value for money?

Or do we unfairly weight our scales by using deceitful tactics, such as inflating the price of our product before we announce a "sale"? Do we say a product is worth a whole lot more than its true value? Living by a code of "accurate weights" - serving the customer well and always giving good value for money - will bring success.

2. Don't make false claims.

Only make promises you can deliver. It's a challenge to authentically market your product - or yourself - without exaggerating and making promises you aren't able to fulfil. Is your claim authentic and deliverable?

Like a north wind that brings unexpected rain
is a sly tongue - which provokes a horrified look.

Proverbs 25:23

When I first read this verse, I couldn't make sense of it. In a hot arid country, surely rain is welcome, even if it is unexpected; so why does the following line refer to a horrified look? What was the metaphor here? I pondered this till I recognised the geography of the region. Then it figured - the mountains are in the North, which means that the rain from a north wind would fall on the other side of the mountain range; the north wind might have appeared to be promising rain, but it never happened!

Unfulfilled promises provoke anger. People will be upset if you don't deliver on the promises you make.

3. Don't trick people into purchasing what they don't need.

Proverbs 5:3 talks about the dangers of "smooth lips". Learning to advertise well is key to success because people won't know about your product unless you advertise. But are you truthfully promoting a product or service worth purchasing?

The mouth of an adulterous woman is a deep pit;

Proverbs 22:14a

Are we in danger of our business being the seductress? Are we luring people to meet our ends, at their expense? Could we be creating a "deep pit" that swallows other people's cash and self-belief?

… and their lips are a snare to their very lives.

Proverbs 18:7b

The word "allurement" is also used to describe a snare - which is baited with something that will entice with treacherous outcomes. Don't use clever words or ploys, such as clickbait, to trap the unwitting.

4. Don't blow your own horn, especially to prominent leaders.

In digital marketing we write our own blurbs about who we are and what we do. And it's a challenge to do this in an authentic way without appearing arrogant.

… to seek one's own glory is not glory.

Proverbs 25:27 NKJV

5. Don't underestimate the power of word of mouth.

The lips of the righteous know what finds favour,

Proverbs 10:32a

When you follow Wisdom's path, you'll create products and services which genuinely attract people - rather than trying to persuade folk to buy something they don't need. And you'll discover how to attract your 'tribe' who are genuinely interested in what you offer. And word of mouth is the best advertisement of all. Happy customers tell others.

When people of influence see we are doing a good job and offering a good product, word spreads exponentially.

6. Don't let social media be your master.

Nir Eyal states seventy-nine per cent of smartphone owners check their device within fifteen minutes of waking every morning.[32] Like sweet foods, social media can be addictive!

If you find honey, eat just enough –
too much of it, and you will vomit.

Proverbs 25:16

Don't allow social media to eat your time. Have a clear strategy of when and how you do your digital marketing, and what you will and won't post. For example, unless your profession is politics, don't post about political issues on your official social media platforms.

Like a city whose walls are broken through
is a person who lacks self-control.

Proverbs 25:28

It is interesting that this is the final verse of the chapter that has so much that is relevant to digital marketing. In both how and when we use social media, the bottom line is self-control!

7. Don't be hasty to publicly denounce others.

Often, we don't know all the facts of a situation. It's easy to make a negative comment about someone else on social media because we don't see the pain we cause. It only takes a minute to type, but it's an indelible record we can't withdraw once we've put it in the public arena.

What you have seen with your eyes
do not bring hastily to court,
for what will you do in the end
if your neighbour puts you to shame?

Proverbs 25:7b-8

Negative comments can backfire. The wise person recognises that attacks on character indicate more about the person who is saying it than the person they're commenting on. Likewise, avoid affirming other people's posts that demean someone's character or promote violence and prejudice.

Don't harm another's reputation. Don't post, repost, share, tweet or retweet anything you are not absolutely certain about. Misquoted or exaggerated information can paint others in a bad light, or stir up hatred or fear.

> *Like a club or a sword or a sharp arrow*
> *is one who gives false testimony against a neighbour.*

Proverbs 25:18

When we use social media to make derogatory comments, we start something that could negatively impact others.

> *Like a maniac shooting*
> *flaming arrows of death*
> *is one who deceives their neighbour*
> *and says, 'I was only joking!'*

Proverbs 26:18-19

Flaming arrows can start a raging fire that isn't easily extinguished – and can cause deadly damage.

For example, there is a big difference between saying,

"I disagree with Joe Soap's opinion."

and

"Joe Soap is scum. He's an idiot."

People behave online in ways they wouldn't dream of behaving if the person they were demeaning was standing in front of them. Avoid attacking people's character or posting anything alarmist. Wisdom chooses courtesy and consideration. Be someone who promotes harmony and hope.

8. Don't resort to cunning, deceitful, manipulative, dishonest, duplicitous, underhand or sneaky behaviours.

Whoever winks maliciously causes grief,

Proverbs 10:10a

When does a person wink? There's the playful wink when people are having fun and there's the malicious wink - indicating to another that you are deliberately deceiving. In the long run, deception never works!

9. Don't trust an incompetent person to handle your digital marketing.

Sending a message by the hands of a fool
is like cutting off one's feet or drinking poison.

Proverbs 26:23

A fool is a person who acts unwisely or imprudently - not showing any care for the consequences of a decision. Be certain of who you employ to do your social media, or you could discover they haven't done what they were contracted to do. Sloppy presentation, grammar or punctuation, or inappropriate posts can damage your brand. Having the wrong person in charge of your digital marketing can be as harmful to your business as cutting off its feet or feeding it poison. It won't get anywhere fast and it might die an untimely death!

10. Don't be over-effusive in your praise of others, it could be misinterpreted.

If anyone loudly blesses their neighbour early in the morning,
it will be taken as a curse.

Proverbs 27:14

Over-the-top effusive statements in praise of others could be viewed with scepticism and distrust.

11. Don't envy those who use aggressive tactics or who promote violence to get rich.

Whenever business marketing aims at making a sale at any cost, the cost is too high.

> *Do not envy the violent*
> *or choose any of their ways.*
>
> Proverbs 3:31

In our digital age, this isn't only about physical violence. How much is the aggression and violence in the way we interact on social media undermining mental health, and at what cost to community well-being?

What about the more subtle ways we attack people's self-esteem - creating messages they are not smart enough / safe enough / cool enough / beautiful enough unless you buy … blah blah, blah!

What violence are we thrusting on our planet by our never-ending promotion of consumerism?

Business success is not true success unless it's creating win-win for all concerned, including Planet Earth.

The Outcome of Unethical Digital Marketing

> *… a perverse tongue will be silenced.*
>
> Proverbs 10:31b

> *Ill-gotten treasures have no lasting value,*
>
> Proverbs 10:2a

> *A false witness will not go unpunished,*
> *and whoever pours out lies will perish.*
>
> Proverbs 19:9

If we resort to making false promises to get a quick sale then our business model has no solid foundation and ultimately there will be dire consequences.

The Power of Digital Marketing

The power of the internet is its mega-magnification impact. It's as though something said softly in a room is amplified so loudly it can be heard throughout the world. This has tremendous power to do good but, likewise, to cause harm. Let's always give value for money and bring a message which refreshes and restores.

Like cold water to a weary soul
is good news from a distant land.

Proverbs 25:25

That's a brilliant 2000-year-old plug for ethical digital marketing:

Any tool can be used for good or bad. It's really the ethics of the artist using it.

John Knoll

Time to reflect:

Take each of the twelve "Don'ts" listed above, flip them over and write each one as a positive "Do" that relates to your digital marketing. For example, 7. "Don't let social media be your master" could become "Social media is my helpful servant."

Which of these twelve pointers most challenges you?

What steps do you need to take to bring this into action in your practice?

So, how do we ensure our business offers a genuine product which people need; and how do we make sure we don't waste our precious resources being sucked dry by other people's get rich scams?

Chapter 19

The Seduction of Get Rich Quick

Every day I receive emails that bombard me with spam – advertising apps I should buy, courses I should sign up for and webinars I should attend. Some of this spamming is obviously snake oil. Here's a warning to beware the lure of the "get rich quick" scammers.

Those who work their land will have abundant food,
but those who chase fantasies will have their fill of poverty.

Proverbs 28:19

Did you ever see the film or read the book *The Field*? Although it's set in a different geography to the context of Proverbs, you see the patient, ongoing and back-breaking work it takes to create an arable field from virgin land. You recognise the ongoing work, year in and year out, of planting crops, tending them and harvesting. There is no such thing as overnight success. Any successful organisation takes time and consistent work to establish, especially in the early stages. Are you chasing elusive butterflies of the imagination or are you *working your land?*

A faithful person will be richly blessed,
but one eager to get rich will not go unpunished.

Proverbs 28:20

Beware the Lure of Bad Business Deals

Perhaps we may be tempted by get-rich-quick promises. Maybe we are lured by power or prestige? What tugs us away from our integrity?

The stingy are eager to get rich
and are unaware that poverty awaits them.

Proverbs 28:22

Beware the seduction of a shady deal which supposedly offers incredible reward. Unethical decisions that we think can be hidden away have a nasty habit of bursting out into the public arena, especially in this era of social-media!

"… I am on the brink of utter ruin in the midst of the whole assembly."

Proverbs 5:14

How many public figures have faced disgrace and been taken down when their indiscretion is leaked to the media!

There is an old expression: "When it sounds too good to be true, it probably is." **What may look like a tempting opportunity might have a nasty sting in the tail.**

… the cords of their sins hold them fast.

Proverbs 5:22b

Okay, "sin" may not be a word in people's everyday vocabulary, but we can still be ensnared (held fast) by our bad choices. The original Hebrew word that is translated as "sin" means to "miss the mark".[33] There are many ways in which we "miss the mark" of creating businesses that are in line with Wisdom's eternal principles, that, at worst, can cause harm and lead to evil outcomes.

To reflect on this Proverb, consider the behaviours that might manacle or ensnare people who are not living by Wisdom's guidelines. Let's avoid the trap!

How to Guard Against Being Seduced into Bad Business Deals

Solomon's description of the adulteress can be a helpful metaphor for any form of seduction we face. He describes the seductress as having "lips like honey".

> *With persuasive words she led him astray;*
> *she seduced him with her smooth talk.*

Proverbs 7:21

What are the honeyed words, the smooth talk of seducers in the business world, which could lure us into making unwise decisions?

> *… her paths wander aimlessly, but she does not know it.*

Proverbs 5:6b

The seducers are out there and they do not have a conscience about the traps they cast. It's our job to be discerning. How do we guard against being unwittingly seduced into bad deals? Let's look at how Solomon's advice regarding the adulteress can be applied to business enchantments:

Tip #1 If you follow seduction, you'll find yourself in trouble you didn't anticipate.

> *… he followed her*
> *like an ox going to the slaughter,*
> *like a deer stepping into a noose.*

Proverbs 7:22

Tip #2 Keep well away from potential trouble.

> *Keep to a path far from her,*
> *do not go near the door of her house,*

Proverbs 5:8

Tip #3 Have clear purposeful goals.

Notice the setting of these verses:

> *… I noticed among the young men,*
> *a youth who had no sense.*
> *He was going down the street near her corner,*
> *walking along in the direction of her house*

Proverbs 7:7,8

The Amplified Bible, Classic Edition describes the young man as "sauntering".

"Strolling" or "sauntering" is walking in a leisurely way. Are we "sauntering" into shady deals because we don't have a clear focus of where and how we're going to reach our goals?

Write down what you desire to achieve, how you plan to do it and by when.

Tip #4 Always act in a way that you don't mind who sees your actions.

> *He was going down the street …*
> *… as the day was fading,*
> *as the dark of night set in.*

Proverbs 7:8a, 9

Solomon tells us it was twilight. In an age without electricity, when he wasn't easily observed, the youth was led into a course of action he may not have made in the clear light of day.

When we act with integrity, we take ownership of our actions; we choose to be in a place of transparency where we have nothing to hide and we won't be ashamed of our transactions.

Tip #5 Make Wisdom your priority.

Wisdom is the key that unlocks success. Solomon's heads his prologue[34] of Proverbs with the caption:

"Exhortations to Embrace Wisdom".

Solomon tells us why Wisdom matters and he also warns us of the dangers we may face. He gives us the route out of seduction's "highway to the grave."[35]

Get-rich-quick practices can lead to disappointing our customers and clients. **When we build our business with integrity, one sure step at a time, we create the quality of product and service that instils loyalty and trust.**

Solomon gives a clarion call to the alternate path:

Does not wisdom call out?
Does not understanding raise her voice?

Proverbs 8:1

Quality is not what happens when what do you do matches your intentions.
It's what happens when what you do matches your customers' expectations.

John Guaspari

Time to reflect:

What might seduce you from being the wise business-person you desire to be?

Which of these five tips most resonates with you and what are you going to do about it?

What difference could that make to your business and to your life?

The ethical path, that leads to true success, is in plain sight, and it is evidenced by our actions. So, what is a core quality that makes our business outstanding?

Chapter 20

Why Generosity Matters

I t's become fashionable in the business world to be a giver to impress others - to make a positive social statement. Success is not just about being generous; it's about *why* we are generous.

Honour the Lord with your wealth,
with the first-fruits of all your crops;
then your barns will be filled to overflowing
And your vats will brim over with new wine.

Proverbs 3:9,10

Solomon states that giving generously honours God. What might this mean? People of the Christian faith regularly pray "Thy Kingdom come" but it seems they seldom reflect on what those words mean. Whilst it is only by the revelation of God's Spirit that we begin to truly understand God's Kingdom, Jesus taught his followers the Lord's Prayer and lived by the code of social justice he declared. He fed the hungry, he healed the sick. He reached out to those in need.

If we look at Christ's example, can we perceive that praying for God's kingdom to come is expressing a heart desire for love, peace, respect, justice and harmony to permeate our world? We need to open our eyes to see the world with compassion and to reach out to those in need.

Do we see ourselves as active participants in creating a better world? When we perceive ourselves as co-creators in bringing God's kingdom to earth, we bring our energy and our resources to the table too.

We make a better world a reality by giving generously. We can financially support charitable causes and also share our expertise and experience with others, including other entrepreneurs who are on the same journey as we are. Are we generous with our resources, and in helping others to connect with people who can support their business venture and life journey? I am where I am today because of the generosity of fellow-travellers on the entrepreneurial quest for success and, of course, it needs to be reciprocal.

It's also about being wise about who you are giving to. What are the causes that give you a sense of excitement? What organisations inspire you to affiliate with them because you believe their work makes a significant difference in this world?

A helpful framework for understanding that people from different backgrounds have a different mindset concerning issues like money, education, possessions, destiny and motivation, is discussed by Danny Silk in *Culture of Honour – Sustaining a Supernatural Environment*. He references the framework proposed by Dr Ruby Payne.[36] Her theory is that some people and communities are trapped in a mindset of poverty, where people see themselves as powerless to bring change. On the other end of the scale are people with a wealth mindset, who have an outlook of abundance and "noblesse oblige" - they see it as their responsibility to support and empower those in need.

It's important to recognise that having money does not automatically free a person from a poverty mindset. Wealthy people can still be trapped in a poverty mindset. On the other hand, people like Mother Theresa, who have little in the way of material possessions, choose to live generously.

Silk is of the opinion that having a mindset of wealth is one of the most important components of bringing heaven to earth. He states,

"The wealthy understand that prosperity must expand if it is to last."

People of a wealth mindset understand that resources are not ends in themselves but are a vehicle to bringing well-being, social justice, liberty, harmony and beauty to all, especially those most in need. And there is a growing awareness in society that we need to secure this not only for our own generation but also for future generations. He describes this "culture of honour" as a practice - a way of being.

Christ set the ultimate example of giving freely of himself, and we honour God, the divine Source who provides abundantly for us, through our generosity. Honouring the Lord isn't only about giving generously; it's also about the attitude with which we give.

~ Am I giving begrudgingly?

~ Am I giving hesitatingly?

~ Am I giving out of guilt rather than a freedom of spirit?

~ Am I giving wisely to causes that have the possibility of making God's Kingdom come to earth?

> *The generous will themselves be blessed,*
> *for they share their food with the poor.*
>
> **Proverbs 22:9**

There have been times in my life when financial giving hasn't been easy. It's hard to give money away when we have financial responsibilities to be met. A generous attitude is about honouring God with our first-fruits - choosing to make it our first priority to give to work that brings his Kingdom to come, rather than giving our leftover coins to charitable causes.

As well as our finances, we can give our time and our talents. Who should we be giving to? We need discernment because there are so many needs.

> *One person gives freely, yet gains even more;*
> *another withholds unduly, but comes to poverty.*
>
> **Proverbs 11:24**

PeopleSpeak: What goes around comes around.

Every man must decide whether he will walk in the light of creative altruism or in the darkness of destructive selfishness.

Martin Luther King, Jr[37]

Time to reflect:

What most challenges you in this chapter? And what do you choose to do about that?

Which organisation or movement is particularly close to your heart?

In what ways can you make a difference in society - and be part of bringing God's kingdom to earth?

We'll chat more about generosity in the section "Be the Difference That Makes the Difference." In our next chapter we'll look at leading the team, which matters to all of us because it's not only employees who are our team.

Chapter 21

Leading Your Team

Solomon had an entourage of helpers. If you are in charge of a palace and an entire kingdom it makes sense you have insight into employment and employees. The same principles can also be applied to working with volunteers or interacting with any other team.

Hire wisely.

It's often said, it's better to hire the person with the ideal personality and character who does not yet have all the qualifications than the person who is more proficient but has a poor temperament. This makes sense, because you can train a person and equip them with the necessary skills, but you can't change their character. Be careful to check out someone you consider hiring before you bring them onto your team. In this day and age, that applies to virtual assistants as much as the face-to-face people in our office.

> *Like an archer who wounds at random*
> *is one who hires a fool or any passer-by.*

Proverbs 26:10

A "fool" - one who doesn't have a moral compass - can do untold damage to your organisation. The thing is, when you employ a fool, even if you put in the effort to help them, they are not going to change their ways.

Though you grind a fool in a mortar,
grinding them like grain with a pestle,
you will not remove their folly from them.

Proverbs 27:22

Try using a pestle and mortar to grind grain. It's ridiculously hard work - the grains somehow keep slipping away and it's an almost impossible task. That's how difficult it is to remove folly from the fool. Their foolishness is ingrained!

Like a thorn-bush in a drunkard's hand
is a proverb in the mouth of a fool.

Proverbs 26:9

Just as a drunkard won't feel the pain of what he's clutching, so the fool won't heed advice. These are graphic descriptions here. The writer ensures we don't miss the point!

As a dog returns to its vomit,
so fools repeat their folly.

Proverbs 26:11

Don't think you are going to change the fool's habits or natural inclinations. The fool is self-opinionated and doesn't think there is anything they need to learn.

Do you see a person wise in their own eyes?
There is more hope for a fool than for him.

Proverbs 26:12

Avoid employing a person who stirs up trouble because they can cause upsets that can rage through your business, causing havoc.

As charcoal to embers and as wood to fire,
so is a quarrelsome person for kindling strife.

Proverbs 26:21

The bottom line is - before you employ someone, assess carefully whether they are likely to integrate well into your team. Unless they can, they won't be able to honour your brand.

Stone is heavy and sand a burden,
but a fool's provocation is heavier than both.

Proverbs 27:3

Don't employ staff who are going to be a burden! To do so is likely to lead to your having to pick up issues that are going to be so heavy you don't want to cart them around.

Be careful who you appoint to senior positions.

People don't quit jobs, people quit managers. Solomon must have noticed the challenge of the wrong person being employed in a senior position because he alludes to it repeatedly.

It is not fitting for a fool to live in luxury -
how much worse for a slave to rule over princes!

Proverbs 19:10

I take this to mean a person with a slave mentality - who is bound by rigid and out-dated rules of what is possible - won't be able to lead your team members who are "royalty"- the ones who dare to dream big dreams and see a greater vision of what could be.

Like snow in summer or rain in harvest,
honour is not fitting for a fool.

Proverbs 26:1

Giving the honour of a management position to one who is not equipped for the position means there will be no long-lasting gain - it will melt away like snow in summer.

Solomon also compares this to rain during harvest. Every farmer knows that out-of-season rain, when the crop should have already come to fruition, can destroy the entire harvest. Solomon is implying that we should rather give honour to those who have earned it.

And here's a metaphor that takes some puzzling:

Like tying a stone in a sling
is the giving of honour to a fool.

Proverbs 26:8

I couldn't figure out this Proverb when I first read it. And then I laughed. *Of course!* You don't tie a stone in a catapult. That would defeat the very purpose of placing the stone in the sling - it is supposed to be a missile. You put it in the sling because you intend it to fulfil a particular purpose. If it is tied, it won't fly when it is released. It won't do what it should when you need it to. Giving honour to a fool is going to hit you in the face! This would have been an image that made sense to Solomon. He had 700 slingshot experts who were so accurate they could "sling a stone at a hair and not miss"[38] O*h! That's why we say "dead accurate"!*

Wisdom for Supporting Employees

As the word "king" could infer a person in a position of authority, so perhaps the word "children" could suggest employees.

Discipline your children, for in that there is hope;
do not be a willing party to their death.

Proverbs 19:18

Discipline is about setting clear guidelines and boundaries. When we set clear limits there is hope because everyone knows what is expected of them. And, because effective discipline is the gift that nurtures self-discipline, you create hope for the future. People will be able to work competently and autonomously. If we do not set clear boundaries, this could lead to their demise from the company - because ultimately no-one is satisfied when there is a lack of clarity about who is responsible for what.

And it is interesting that the very next verse is about dealing with anger:

A hot-tempered person must pay the penalty;
rescue them, and you will have to do it again.

Proverbs 19:19

A hot-temper is about a lack of self-control, which is a boundary issue. If we allow our own temper, or that of others, to boil over there is always a price to pay in relationships. And the thing is emotions are contagious, so as a leader it is not just how well-skilled a person might be for the job; it's important to be thinking about how the person might impact the socio-emotional climate of your work environment.

Do not make friends with a hot-tempered person,
do not associate with one easily angered,
or you may learn their ways
and get yourself ensnared.

Proverbs 22:24,25

Similarly, we could apply the verse to the newbie on the team, if we give a wider interpretation of "children" as those without experience.

Start children off on the way they should go,
and even when they are old they will not turn from it.

Proverbs 22:6

As the team leader, are you creating the environment for everyone to thrive, right from the outset?

Whoever sows injustice reaps calamity,
and the rod they wield in fury will be broken.

Proverbs 22:8

Again, let's see this as a metaphor. Obviously, we are not going to resort to physical punishment but do we take firm measures when someone's behaviour is disrespectful of others? This matters because there are always others who are observing. People in the team learn how to behave by what we allow.

Flog a mocker, and the simple will learn prudence;
rebuke the discerning, and they will gain knowledge.

Proverbs 19:25[39]

We'll talk more about how to respond to challenging behaviours when we discuss dealing with anger and conflict. When we create an environment where people love to work - including yourself - everyone thrives and this means your business thrives too.

In the presence of greatness, pettiness disappears.
In the absence of a great dream, pettiness prevails.

Peter M. Senge

Time to reflect:

What are the qualities you most value in your team members?

What have you put in place to ensure you create a sense of team - even if you are a team of one?

How can you build a greater sense of team?

What difference could that make to your business and to your life?

Proverbs 27:18 states that the one who guards a fig tree will eat its fruit. Are we guarding the relationships we value, including the relationships with our employees, customers and clients? More on this in the next chapter on why ethics in business are the foundation to success.

Chapter 22

Ethics in Business - the Foundation of Success

A crooked stick or a crooked path is not straight. A crooked stick won't make a good walking stick and a crooked path can make the route frustrating and much longer.

Whoever walks in integrity walks securely,
but whoever takes crooked paths will be found out.

Proverbs 10:9

The word "crooked" has two different meanings. It can mean "not straight" or "twisted", and it can mean "questionable" or "devious". Perhaps these meanings are more closely linked than we realise! If people choose devious ways the path won't be straight, and over time it mis-shapes their character and their personality.

Are we living with integrity and avoiding the "crooked path"? For each of us, it's a daily choice.

Proverbs are a great code of conduct for ethical business. Here is what I glean:

1. Obey the laws of the land.

Whoever keeps commandments keeps their life,
but whoever shows contempt for their ways will die.

Proverbs 19:16

Perhaps we won't physically die but, ultimately, our organisation will die if we do not keep to the law.

2. Always be trustworthy.

When people know your name can be trusted they will return to your business and they will be happy to recommend you to their friends.

Like a broken tooth or a lame foot
is reliance on the unfaithful in a time of trouble.

Proverbs 25:19

I laugh at the simile of the broken tooth because I recently had a back tooth extracted, after months of difficulty with it. I have had an ongoing feeling of malaise because of this tooth. It is amazing how one little thing can upset the well-being and equilibrium of an entire system. Deal immediately with the "broken tooth" or "lame foot" in your workplace so that your team and customers know they can trust you.

3. Always speak for truth. Never give false evidence.

Those living in the Republic of Ireland will remember the Maurice McCabe case - the Garda whistle-blower who endured an ongoing, coordinated smear campaign. McCabe's reputation was torn apart by people whom the public thought they could trust. The story was big news and it took a decade before McCabe was vindicated. He and his wife stood for truth despite the false allegations and vicious maligning. No matter whether it is in our personal lives or the public domain the collateral damage of eroded trust is beyond any price tag.

… surely to flog honest officials is not right.

Proverbs 17:26b

Whistle blowers are honest officials who often get "flogged". And, in our day and age, ostracisation can be mega-magnified through social media. Are we standing for ethical and fair practices and challenging the system when a blind eye is turned to corruption or malpractice? And are we creating a society built on a foundation of honesty and truth?

*Do not testify against your neighbour without cause –
would you use your lips to mislead?*

Proverbs 24:28

Whether it's making claims about a person or about your product, only make statements you can substantiate.

4. Treat everyone fairly.

*It is not good to be partial to the wicked
and so deprive the innocent of justice.*

Proverbs 18:5

Treating everyone well matters in our own business practices, but also consider the impact of those from whom we purchase. If, for instance, we buy goods from companies that have a reputation for exploiting their employees, we are supporting unethical practice. **Cheap is not cheap if it is at someone else's expense.** Are we encouraging fair trade and right-living by giving our business to ethical companies?

5. Keep to the standards of ethical practice, no matter how great the temptation.

> *Better a little with righteousness*
> *than much gain with injustice.*
>
> **Proverbs 16:8**

It can be tempting to cut corners or to talk ourselves into making an unethical choice, especially if we are in a challenging situation, or there is the temptation of a big win. When we trust Wisdom's guidance, we will focus on doing the right thing, knowing that everything will work out for the best in the greater scheme of things.

6. Always choose to do the right thing.

In every situation we have a choice to make and our choice either leads us in the direction we want, or leads us into unfortunate circumstances. As indicated in Proverbs 22:5, there are paths that will lead to "snares and pitfalls" that we need to stay well away from.

> *The highway of the upright avoids evil;*
>
> **Proverbs 16:17a**

Solomon also offers pertinent advice to those who inherit the family business.

> *Whoever robs their father and drives out their mother*
> *is a child who brings shame and disgrace.*
>
> **Proverbs 19:26**

7. Be very certain of a person's character before standing surety for them.

Whilst we may not stand surety for a stranger by underwriting a financial agreement, we also need to consider that giving a reference for a person is a form of standing surety.

Whoever puts up security for a stranger will surely suffer,

Proverbs 11:15a

8. Live your integrity from the inside out.

People appreciate honesty.

An honest answer
is like a kiss on the lips.

Proverbs 24:26

Likewise, Proverbs 10:18 warns against concealing hatred with lying lips. Ethical business starts with our personal behaviour.

9. Live sustainably and create a business that upholds sustainability.

Death and Destruction are never satisfied,
and neither are human eyes.

Proverbs 27:20

This verse reminds me of a challenge Sage Lavine gives in her book *Women Rocking Business*. She visited the indigenous Achuar people in Ecuador, who are part of the Pachamama Alliance. These women are taking a stand for ethical living that steps away from egoic power and consumerism; they are calling for social justice, sustainability and spiritual fulfilment. And here's the thing - the women in this tribe tell their men, "Enough!" Sage describes how these women see pictures of our huge cities and ask,

"Why haven't the women stood up and said, 'Stop'?"[40]

Our Western world has drifted into chaos and danger because we did not heed Solomon's observation that our human eyes are never satisfied. Our consumer-driven society is always calling out for more. What will it take for us, as a society, to realise that we need to create a sustainable economy? Our civilisation will crumble if we do not know when to stop our relentless depletion of Nature's resources. See also chapters on "Digital Marketing" and "Social Justice".

10. Always stand for justice.

The [king's] mouth does not betray justice.

Proverbs 16:10b

As successful business people we have the power to make a difference. Let's speak out for wellbeing, equality and justice, especially for those who cannot speak for themselves.

11. In every part of your personal and business life, live in a way that upholds your good reputation.

A good name is more desirable than great riches;

Proverbs 22:1a

Ethical business is not an optional plug-in. It is the motherboard of being. There is no lasting success without ethical business.

The righteousness of the upright delivers them,

Proverbs 11:6a

*To lead without a title is to derive your power within the organisation
not from your position but from your competence, effectiveness, relationships,
excellence, innovation and ethics.*

Robin S Sharma

Time to reflect:

Which of these pointers most challenges you?

What do you choose to do about that?

What difference could that make to your business and your life?

In a later chapter we'll look at how we are called to be champions for social justice. We'll be able to make a much bigger difference in the world when we have the resources of a thriving business. So, what might this journey to success look like?

Chapter 23
Going for Gold

In many of the Indiana Jones movies the ancient edifice tears apart and disintegrates when its treasure is removed. Likewise, businesses catastrophically collapse when their core values are removed. Or perhaps there never was a strong ethical foundation - and when something earth-shattering happens the business implodes, often with serious consequences socially or ecologically.

In some third-world countries, earthquake damage has been calamitous owing to lack of regulation of building standards. An insufficient amount of cement was used in construction, which caused buildings to collapse and hence the huge devastation and loss of life. Similarly, the luxury liner Titanic was fated because the company management had cut costs by not using a superior quality steel in building her hull,[41] that could probably have withstood the damage of an iceberg. The decision-makers put profit before people's safety.

Building a business without sound values is like building a city with substandard cement or a ship with inferior grade steel. The outer structure might appear sturdy but it will be ravaged by the pressures and shifts that impact the economy. Let's take a quick recap on how to ignite your business success.

In this section we've examined the importance of creating your elevator pitch; of knowing why, what and who your business is for. Crafting a well-thought elevator pitch is helpful for your would-be customers and it also helps you to gain a clearer picture of your organisation's purpose.

We have looked at tips for successful digital marketing success and the temptation of get-rich-quick offers. Building a solid, financially viable business takes time and consistent effort. Beware the lure of bad business deals. It's important to determine what's genuinely worth the investment. We need the cement of Wisdom and understanding to build the business that will last.

Stop listening to instruction, my son,
and you will stray from the words of knowledge.

Proverbs 19: 27[42]

Part of that cement is generosity in supporting others on their life journey - not only financially but also offering time, resources, and connections that support others. And an attitude of generosity builds your team. Your business will only thrive as well as your team thrives, and your team will thrive when they know you have their well-being at heart. **Successful business is built on trust, and trust is established on a core foundation of solid values.** That doesn't mean things will always go as we hope. So, what to do when business doesn't go smoothly?

When Business Doesn't Go Smoothly

Chapter 24

When Things Are Beyond Your Control

As a writer I am blessed with a vivid imagination. Great for writing. Not so great for living, especially if coupled with anxiety. Imagination feeds anxiety and anxiety feeds imagination!

Recently, I had booked my flight for a speaking contract a couple of weeks away. But the forecast threatened a band of severe winter weather heading in. "The Beast from The East" - the newspapers were spreading alarm. *What if the flight is cancelled? What if I can't get there?* Here's Wisdom from this ancient biblical text:

> *In their hearts humans plan their course,*
> *but the Lord establishes their steps.*
>
> **Proverbs 16:9**

If we are walking in Wisdom, we don't need to be anxious; the LORD determines our steps, even though we plan our path. We do our part - and then trust God to work it out, despite the circumstances that are beyond our control! Even when things don't work out as we think they should, there's a greater plan unfolding.

One of the biggest challenges to my peace of mind is that I tell God my worries but then grab them back again. If I am genuinely seeking Wisdom, then I trust God's assurances. I need to trust that there is a divine plan unfolding. (The weather conditions were fine for travelling!)

The horse is made ready for the day of battle,
but victory rests with the LORD.

Proverbs 21:31

At times, building a business can feel like a roller-coaster or clinging to a precarious cliff face, and anxiety or panic can threaten to overwhelm. There will be challenges along the way but these are often where the growth opportunity lies - for oneself and for the organisation.

Commit to the LORD whatever you do,
and he will establish your plans.

Proverbs 16:3

If you are anything like me, learning to trust God is an ongoing journey. Just yesterday, in preparing for a parenting workshop I wrote, "It's time to take the 'steering wheel' and put anxiety in the back seat." The same can be said for every business venture too. **When we believe there is a divine plan unfolding and trust that our success is in God's hands, it is easier to stop anxiety grabbing control.**

Imagine how much easier it would be to succeed in life if you were constantly expecting
the world to support you and bring you opportunity.

Jack Canfield

Time to reflect:

What causes you the most anxiety regarding your business?

What key thought most resonates with you in this chapter?

What part do you need to undertake, and what do you need to leave to God?

It's going to be easier to let go of anxiety when we choose colleagues and companions who inspire and motivate us. So how do friends and colleagues impact our business success?

Chapter 25

Who Do You Hang Out With?

What comes first in a book matters, especially in an instruction manual. There are certain things to get right first, before we proceed! And, to paraphrase one of Solomon's guidelines, "Be careful who you hang out with." [43]

Don't associate with the "wish-we's" but with the achievers and with those who are serious about their work. Align yourself with the successful. We all desire peer acceptance - but *who* do we choose as our peers? Not only our face-to face colleagues - who do we hang out with online? Whose company are we keeping in what we choose to view or read? Be it actual friends, or virtual acquaintances - choose wisely.

When we hang out with the wrong companions, there are long-term consequences. Solomon doesn't mince his words. He calls them "fools".

I equate "fool" with "idiot" or "simpleton" but when I check out the meaning of "fool" I discover it describes one who is morally deficient.[44] That's a whole different ball-game to being a simpleton. With this definition we can all think of politicians and other public figures who are "fools". The bottom line: Don't hang out with the morally deficient.

... the complacency of fools will destroy them;

Proverbs 1:32b

"Complacency" is defined as:

"a feeling of smug or uncritical satisfaction with oneself or one's achievements."[45]

So, this verse could read:

"The smugness of people who ignore moral and ethical principles will destroy them."

How much of the social mess in the world - corruption, abuse, social injustice, war mongering - would be eliminated if we didn't give centre-stage to the fools!

And it's a greater challenge because behaviours, attitudes and emotions are contagious.

> *Do not make friends with a hot-tempered person,*
> *do not associate with one easily angered,*
> *or you may learn their ways*
> *and get yourself ensnared.*
>
> **Proverbs 22:24,25**

And watch out for those who over-indulge in extravagant lifestyles because their lifestyle choices will lead to ruin.

> *... do not join those who drink too much wine*
> *or gorge themselves on meat,*
> *for drunkards and gluttons become poor,*
> *and drowsiness clothes them in rags.*
>
> **Proverbs 23:20-21**

The attitudes, generosity or stinginess of those we hang out with can also impact us.

> *Do not eat the food of a stingy host. ...*
> *You will vomit up the little you have eaten...*
>
> **Proverbs 23:6a,8b**

And with fools, the level of conversation is entirely different.

> *Do not speak with fools*
> *for they will scorn your prudent words.*
>
> **Proverbs 23:9**

Perhaps we "speak with fools" when we watch mindless TV, or waste time on trivial social media interactions. It's easy to get caught up in conversations that aren't helping us towards our goals of living fully and wisely. See also the chapter "Beware the Get-Rich-Quick Scam".

Some would argue you're as successful as the company you keep.

> *Certainly there is a connection between our friends and who we are.*
>
> **Simon Sinek**

Time to reflect:

Who do you hang out with, face-to-face and online?

Whose company do you need to set yourself free from if you want your business to flourish?

Whose company uplifts and energises you?

What practical steps do you need to take today to start making this happen?

Recognising that successful people hang out with successful people, what is a key attribute to creating lasting success?

Chapter 26
The Balancing Act

Don't seek wealth - seek Wisdom. When we focus on getting rich, we will end up chasing the wrong goals that won't lead us to our most fulfilling destination. What we focus on is what we get. Getting rich sounds as if it is the dream - but at what cost, if this is our sole aim? What is Wisdom saying to us?

> *Do not wear yourself out to get rich;*
>
> **Proverbs 23:4a**

True wealth isn't money. Money can buy you freedom, comfort and the luxury of travel. But money in itself cannot buy you security or happiness. Wealth is much more than money. True wealth is living fully - it's about a life that is balanced.

Life Out of Balance - Beware Addictions and Excesses

> *Wine is a mocker and beer a brawler;*
> *whoever is led astray by them is not wise.*
>
> **Proverbs 20:1**

Even if drink is not your challenge, Proverbs 23:29-35 gives a clear description of addiction - the allurement and danger that can easily attract. It's easy to think this doesn't apply to us, but each of us has our own weak points. Understanding the pattern of an addiction can help us to avoid the trap, or recognise what might be unfolding for someone else. I invite you to take a few moments to read and reflect on these verses. It's intriguing to notice the pattern of addictive behaviour that unfolds in these verses.

The Desire

Proverbs 23:31 describes the person gazing at the red wine, sparkling in its cup. It has your attention - you are not 'glancing' – you are 'gazing'!

Just one sip …

This verse continues to say that it draws you in - the enjoyment: "it goes down smoothly".

It impacts your behaviour.

Then in Proverbs 23:33 it describes that your eyes see "strange sights" and your mind imagines "confusing things".

You are unaware of the harm it is causing you.

What a powerful picture Solomon gives in Proverbs 23:34. He describes a person on high seas, lying on top the rigging who says, "I'm fine!"

They are totally unaware of the huge danger they are facing. If you've ever watched a movie with someone in the rigging of a boat in a storm, they are not "lying around" - they are hanging on for dear life! As the boat pitches in the waves, everything is swinging violently from one extreme to another, and they have no control. In other words, when stormy times hit, the addicted person isn't at the helm.

The allurement becomes an addiction.

The road of gleaming red, seductive wine can lead to alcoholism:

When will I wake up so I can find another drink?

Proverbs 23:35b

Eventually the addiction takes its toll.

Whether it is drink, or any other addiction, the pattern is here in these verses: we are tempted to linger on what attracts us; it alters our behaviour and confuses our clear thinking. We feel set free from our everyday challenges and we don't feel the pain - until its poison affects our whole system.

> *Who has woe, sorrow and strife? Who has complaints?*
> *Who has needless bruises? Who has bloodshot eyes?*
>
> Proverbs 23:29

The addict suffers the consequences described, emotionally and socially. If we fall into the trap, we may suffer, physically and psychologically. And by then it may be too late.

> *In the end it bites like a snake and poisons like a viper.*
>
> Proverbs 23:32

What addictions are we prone to: our smartphones, social media, computer, games, alcohol, drugs, sex, pornography, consumerism, unhealthy relationships, work? There's a consequence physically, emotionally and socially. And when we recognise the pattern we can choose differently. Wisdom leads the way to happier outcomes. It's all about balance.

Why Does Balance Matter?

Imagine if you were drawing your last conscious breaths on this earth, what choices do you wish you'd made? What matters most? Solomon brings our attention to the things that matter most in life:

> *What a person desires is unfailing love;*
>
> Proverbs 19:22a

We all need caring relationships. Balance between our work and other activities is essential for our overall health. We can't be tuned-in and at our most creative when we're on a wobble because our lives are out of balance; it impacts our ability to live fully and work well. And if work isn't going well then finances aren't going well. **Life out of balance is like trying to ride a bicycle with a buckled wheel - you won't get anywhere fast and you're likely to take a tumble.** When we are over-tired and over-worked and financially stressed, we're likely to be snappy with the ones we care about the most. And we won't have positive energy in our working relationships with clients, colleagues and team members.

Balance impacts our happiness levels too.

balance = order = harmony = feel good = happiness

Happiness is not a goal but it is the natural by-product when we live wisely.

> *A cheerful heart is good medicine*
> *but a crushed spirit dries up the bones.*
>
> **Proverbs 17:22**

So, in which direction are we headed?

> *The one who gets wisdom loves life;*
>
> **Proverbs 19:8a**

The choice is ours. We all have only 24 hours in a day. It's how we choose to use them that counts. Are we going to fall into the snare of addictive habits, or are we going to create the balance in our lives that makes life a journey we'll be glad we made?

> *In the paths of the wicked are snares and pitfalls,*
> *but those who would preserve their life stay far from them.*
>
> **Proverbs 22:5**

Here's another angle on this same verse. The words "preserve their life" are translated differently. Proverbs 22:5 ESV[46] states those who would *guard their souls* stay far from the snares and pitfalls. This translation suggests it's not only about our physical life in the here and now - but it is our soul-journey too.

> *We are not physical beings on a spiritual journey;*
> *we are spiritual beings on a physical journey.*
>
> Pierre Teilhard de Chardin

The busy-ness of business can overtake us, crowding out other things that matter. To live lives we enjoy, we need to keep balance in our lives.

> *Happiness is not a matter of intensity*
> *but of balance and order and rhythm and harmony.*
>
> Thomas Merton

Time to reflect:

What area of your life do you most need to address to gain better balance?

What might you choose to cut back?

What might you choose to increase?

What habit might you succumb to, that could become an addiction?

If you are facing an addiction challenge, what help do you need to overcome it?

What is the one small doable step you can do today to bring more balance into your life?

I know I'm on the journey, but it's easy for me to get side-tracked with things that gobble my time and suck my energy. **When we take control of our habits, then our business and our life transforms from cacophony to symphony.** So how do we stop laziness and procrastination robbing us of time?

Chapter 27

Laziness and Procrastination

Don't be a sluggard! As I read Proverbs 24:30 describing the circumstances of a sluggard I pondered on what alternative word we'd use today. Sluggard is not a word we ordinarily relate to.

This question was still running through my mind when I was on our monthly Biz Rocking Gals online meeting.

"I've been feeling really sluggish," commented one member.

Aha! Sluggard … sluggish … like a slug … getting nowhere fast. But what was an alternative noun? A lay-about? Almost all my journalling about Proverbs has been by hand but, for some unknown reason, the following morning I used the laptop. As I typed, the autocorrect changed "sluggard" to "slacker".

Slacker. That's it!

How Laziness Undermines Our Business

> *I went past the fields of the sluggard,*
> *past the vineyard of someone who has no sense;*
> *thorns had come up everywhere,*
> *the ground was covered with weeds,*
> *and the stone wall was in ruins.*

> Proverbs 24:30-31

The sluggard, or slacker, doesn't deal with issues in their early stages - and soon untended troubles grow into brambles. Ignore weeds for a few seasons and, without regular maintenance, a garden will be overgrown. The longer issues are left unattended, the bigger they become; the greater and more daunting the tasks!

Yes, there will be days when we feel sluggish. But do we get up and do the work anyway? One of the biggest threats to success is when we lack consistency in carrying through our plans. Sometimes we swap between hare and tortoise behaviours rather than create a constant routine and work habit. Ever since I started park-running, I've learnt that slow and steady does better than mad dashes and slowdowns.

A little sleep, a little slumber,
a little folding of the hands to rest –
and poverty will come on you like a bandit
and scarcity like an armed man.

Proverbs 24:33, 34

The slacker is the one most prone to procrastination and distraction. Perhaps today Solomon might have written: "A little sleep, a little slumber, a little checking of the social media …"

And notice the images: "and poverty will come on you like a bandit and scarcity like an armed man." A bandit is going to steal away what's precious to you without warning, when you least expect it; There will be no time to prepare!

Laziness brings on deep sleep,

Proverbs 19:15a

If a person is deeply asleep, they aren't aware of what's going on around them. They won't be alert for the signs of danger - they won't be observing the key metrics of their business, the shifts in the social and economic climate - which means they won't protect themselves from danger and they could also miss opportunities.

What Causes Laziness

I'm not lazy; I wouldn't classify myself as a slacker, but I am a master at self-distraction and procrastination. I know the antidote to this is having a clear plan of what I need to achieve right now, and working towards my goals. So why do I still fall into the trap?

Laziness, or slacking, comes from lack of ambition or from overwhelm.

Motivation ebbs when we lose sight of our purpose and the excitement of why we are doing what we are doing. If we're battling with laziness or procrastination perhaps it's time to re-examine whether our heart is in this business, and discover what's needed to get back on track.

Perhaps we are slacking because we are fearful we won't achieve our big dream. Or perhaps we are fearful of success itself.

> *The sluggard says, 'There's a lion outside!*
> *I'll be killed in the public square!'*
>
> Proverbs 22:13

Maybe acting sluggishly is sometimes driven by our fear.

As I type this, I notice the words, "I'll be killed in the public square."

Hello – lions are not normally found in public squares!

Isn't this the beast in our minds that roars:

"What will other people say if I mess up? Will they eat me alive?"

Or perhaps our procrastination and slacking is about the fear,

"What will people say if I'm hugely successful?"

The Outcomes of Laziness

And the thing is, slacking impacts others.

> *As vinegar to the teeth and smoke to the eyes,*
> *so are sluggards to those who send them.*
>
> Proverbs 10:26

These are strong images of irritation. When the slacker doesn't come through with what's needed in time, it impacts other team members' ability to get on with the job. It smashes our goals and our relationships with customers or clients when the slacker fails to complete what they were asked to do.

> *… the shiftless go hungry.*
>
> Proverbs 19:15b

The lazy go hungry because there is no reaping of reward if the seeds aren't sown and consistently tended. If a good work ethic isn't upheld, the bottom line is "no work, no pay." We won't create successful businesses without putting in the effort. Slacker or consistent worker? It's your choice. What's stopping you?

How to Overcome Sluggardly Habits[47]

The slacker procrastinates, thinking, "Maybe tomorrow I'll start."

That often sounds like an *"If only…"*:

"If only I had the money to …"

"If only I had the time to …"

"If only I had the education …"

"If only" is a dream world. It doesn't exist. The place to start your journey is the place you are in right now. It's time to get moving!

I admit, I allow myself to get distracted when I feel anxious about taking on something I'm not sure how to do - when I am fearful a task is too big, or if it's something I'm not good at doing - like learning new technology. Here are a few things that help me to get through tasks I don't want to do.

1. Chunking

Break the job into bite-size pieces. But having said that, don't leave it so long to come back to the next chunk that you can't remember where you were in the task or have to spend time setting up again.

2. Bundling

This is almost the opposite of chunking, It's helpful to plan which jobs need doing in the same location, with the same tools, or using the same headspace, and bundling these together. For example, to record a series of videos for a training course all at one time, or to set aside a block of time to handle the end of month finances. This is a time-saver because you're all set up for the job, and it's easier to power through by keeping your head in that space.

3. Action

At times I procrastinate because I'm not sure how to do a task. Fear stops me - but when I overcome inertia and start doing the job step by step, I start to figure out what's needed.

With action comes clarity.

Sage Lavine[48]

As I type these words, I recognise the power of the Nike slogan. Anyone who is setting the dream to take on their first marathon knows they have to lace their shoes and take that first step towards success.

Whatever the task, don't wait for clarity - do it, then clarity comes!

Those who work their land will have abundant food,

Proverbs 28:19a

The most difficult thing is the decision to act, the rest is mere tenacity.
The fears are paper tigers.

Amelia Earhart

Time to reflect:

What are you most afraid of in developing your business?

What aspect of your work habits might be sabotaging your progress?

What is the one doable action you can take today to move towards greater clarity?

But what if a lack of self-belief is blocking us from moving forward with our business dreams?

Chapter 28
How to Be a Transformer

As an on-line educator and an author, I sometimes receive an email or a social media post commenting on how my work has helped people. That is so uplifting - my heart swells and it builds my confidence. My work can make a difference! But not everyone who reads my books agrees with my perspective. Every now and then somebody takes a verbal swing at me that knocks me off balance. Other people's comments or behaviour can dent our self-belief. I guess Solomon wouldn't have written about this, if he hadn't experienced it too:

> *Like a fluttering sparrow or a darting swallow,*
> *an undeserved curse does not come to rest.*
>
> **Proverbs 26:2**

When unfairly criticised, it's hard to remember that critic's behaviour is about them and my response is about me. So, don't hang on to upsetting comments. Let them go. Don't worry about those who badmouth you if you know you are living in integrity.

The challenge is to live your life fully, regardless of what others might say. But how can you measure how you are doing? Let's look at the practical steps of applying Wisdom in Proverbs 2:7-10. I notice an "If ... then ..." pattern in these verses.

> *He holds success in store for the upright,*
> *he is a shield to those whose way of life is blameless.*
>
> **Proverbs 2:7**

If your life is upright, then you will find success.

If your walk is blameless - untarnished, above reproach, beyond criticism, above suspicion - then God is your shield. God will protect and safeguard you.

> *…he guards the course of the just*
> *and protects the way of his faithful ones.*
>
> **Proverbs 2:8**

If your course is just - if you have a concern for peace, a genuine respect for people, a lack of prejudice, if you are open-minded, if you act with integrity, are trustworthy and incorruptible - then God will guard your path (the way you are heading).

Take note - it doesn't say every step of the way will be easy, but that God will protect you so you can keep on course.

If you remain faithful, loyal and devoted to what you are divinely called - if you are constant, unswerving, steadfast, dedicated, committed - then God will protect the way.

I read these verses and think about how challenging it can be to create a successful business. Several years ago, an accountant said to me,

"Why don't you close the business - it would be so much easier!"

Noooooooooo! My work needs to happen!

On days when my work hasn't made financial sense, when I feel overwhelmed and when it would be easy to give up, I keep going because I believe I am called to support people, and especially parents, to think more clearly and connect more compassionately.

Christopher Columbus, the explorer who discovered a route from Europe to America, again comes to my mind. His crew threatened mutiny for fear of plummeting off the edge of the world. They had gone beyond what they dreamed was possible - and fear is often overwhelming when we are out of our comfort zone. Columbus held onto his vision, adjusted his direction and persuaded his crew to give the journey a little longer. He promised they would turn back if they didn't sight land in the next couple of days. And two days later they spotted the "New Land". [49]

Belief gives the courage to keep going even when it isn't easy. What would I miss out on if I turned back and did not steadfastly hold my course, even when things are stormy or frustratingly slow? I want to be a transformer! I want to do my part to make this world a happier, healthier place.

The prospect of the righteous is joy,

Proverbs 10:28a

I perceive that Solomon understood our human habit of doubting ourselves - and he gives encouragement to look to the Source who is so much greater than ourselves. But we still need to do our part.

To recap, these verses indicate that if we act in a way that is blameless and just, and are faithful to what we are called to do, victory will be in store, because God will shield and protect our way. And then we will understand what is right and fair. (Proverbs 2:10) We will know the direction to take - and what paths not to take - because Wisdom will enter our hearts.

In the next chapter we'll look at how to persevere in the face of challenge.

Know also that wisdom is like honey for you:
if you find it, there is future hope for you,
and your hope will not be cut off.

Proverbs 24:14

In these ancient biblical times, it would have taken keen observation, persistence and courage to find honey. Being a transformer becomes so much easier when we are aware God is guarding our course and protecting our way - as we follow our life's calling to the best of our ability. He is looking out for us so we have no need for stress, anxiety or fear.

The spirit does not rest until it fulfils the soul's calling.

Source unknown

Time to reflect:

What is your big dream?

What reassures you in times of self-doubt?

What gives you courage and self-belief when the going is tough?

What difference could that make to your business and to your life?

The mightiest of mighties has the divine power to guide and protect us all the way through to achieving our Final Quest. But what to do when failure comes our way?

Chapter 29

Persevering in the Face of Failure

A few years ago, whilst I was on a long-haul flight, I listened to the audiobook *Unwritten: Reinvent Tomorrow* by Jack Delosa.[50] It describes how to live a life that aligns with your purpose. I was struck by his description of Elon Musk's audacious dreams and his tenacity. And this was years before Musk launched his SpaceX project. Despite his huge earnings, at times he has teetered on the brink of bankruptcy because of his huge investment in his next project.

We can sometimes think it's easy for the successful people - without realising the challenges that have confronted them along the way. They have had the courage and determination to follow their dreams, despite issues that would have overwhelmed almost every other human being. Challenges are part of the entrepreneurial journey.

If you falter in a time of trouble
how small is your strength!

Proverbs 24:10

The Challenge of Failure

I was thinking that Solomon does not say anything about failure when this verse caught my eye:

A person's wisdom yields patience;
it is to one's glory to overlook an offence.

Proverbs 19:11

Rather than focusing on the act of failing, Solomon emphasised offering guidance and exhortation, with an attitude of patience, a willingness to overlook and forgive. He encourages us to recalibrate; and why would he encourage us to do that unless he was aware that, at times, something was amiss?

Many people take failure as an "offence" – perceiving failure as having done something wrong that will cause distress. But failure is the way we learn what's not working, and that's how we figure out how to do things differently. It's to our "glory" - we shine! - when we don't get hung up on failure, whether it's ours or someone else's.

When we, as business leaders, emulate Solomon's open attitude, there will be no need for failure to be concealed. Transparency in the workplace will naturally evolve, as the team experiences that it's okay to make mistakes, to share what has happened, and figure out what you need to do differently. These are teams where trust, creativity and innovation thrive!

This is a call to own where we have missed the mark ourselves, and grow because of the awarenesses we have gained. Do we give that same understanding to ourselves, as well as our team - do we admit our failure and learn from it? When we fail, we learn how to do things better. Failure is essential to gaining Wisdom - which is essential to creating success.

Solomon was an experienced business person. He knew failure would happen sometimes and it wouldn't always be easy.

For though the righteous fall seven times, they rise again …

Proverbs 24:16a

Peoplespeak: It's okay to make mistakes - that's part of the journey.

I read of an example of two jugglers: one juggles five balls; the other juggles twelve. Who do you think is the better juggler? Of course, it's the one who can juggle twelve balls.

And who has dropped the most balls? The one who juggles twelve balls! The greater the challenge we take, the more likely we are to drop some balls along the way. To move beyond the mundane and ordinary we stretch ourselves - and we will make mistakes. We need to be okay with that and not see it as "failure", but as a learning experience.

And for business to thrive, we need the same mindset regarding our team members. If a mistake is frowned upon or punished - seen as "folly" - people's natural inclination is to not own up or to shift the blame to someone else, which means the opportunity for gaining new insights is lost.

Create a climate that encourages everyone to see failure as an opportunity for exploration:

"That's interesting? What can we learn from this? What can we do differently next time?"

Character cannot be developed in ease and quiet. Only through experience of trial and suffering can the soul be strengthened, ambition inspired, and success achieved.

Helen Keller

We need to persevere - to push through when the going is tough. We need courage to look our failures in the face. It takes patience, commitment, courage and perseverance to get to *Awesome!*

The road to success is always under construction.

Arnold Palmer

Time to reflect:

What are the most significant "failures" you have experienced?

What is the greatest learning you have taken from those experiences?

If God is nudging you to a new insight about those experiences, what might that be?

What difference could that make to your business and to your life?

Failure can teach us a better way of doing things. But how do we keep moving forward despite the challenges?

Chapter 30

Why Self-Discipline is Pivotal for Success

Is there any entrepreneur who hasn't wished they could clone themselves! There are always new skills to learn and more tasks to be done, no matter what the line of work.

We are continually figuring out what's needed. With every new stage of development and every success we encounter new challenges. Self-discipline is the lubrication that eases the work - that creates systems to make it happen. But many of us have a resistance to discipline because from our earliest days we have equated discipline to unpleasant interactions and consequences. Perhaps learning effective self-discipline starts with rethinking our understanding of discipline.

Here's how Solomon introduces the topic in the opening chapters of Proverbs:

> *My son, do not despise the LORD's discipline*
> *and do not resent his rebuke,*
> *because the LORD disciplines those he loves,*
> *as a father the son he delights in.*

Proverbs 3:11,12

In our childhood, many of us gained an impression of God as a remote figure in the clouds; a fiery threatening bully who is going to punish our every mistake.

~ What if we have misunderstood how God wants to be in relationship with us?

~ How does it influence our view of self-discipline if we perceive God as compassionate and wanting to offer guidance for us to thrive?

~ How might a different view of discipline impact our relationship with self and with others?

What if we, as a society, are confused by the words "punishment" and "discipline"? Look up their definitions – currently these two words are used interchangeably in almost every English dictionary. But I see discipline as something very different from punishment.

What We Can Learn from Neuroscience About Punishment and Discipline

Punishment

Punishment is something a more powerful person imposes on us; it triggers the fight or flight mode in our brains. Think of a child who is punished; they are likely to fight back: *"It's not fair. I hate you."* Or otherwise the child goes into flight mode – perhaps running sobbing to their room. As adults we are also triggered when we sense a punishing attitude – even from ourselves.

When we are fearful of punishment we don't think clearly or logically and we are in a high-alert reactive mode.

When we think of self-discipline in this light, we are likely to fight back, or duck and dive our responsibilities - *"I'm too busy / stressed without doing anything else!"*

But discipline that is based on healthy mutual respect evokes a different response.

Discipline

Discipline is based on love and nurtures the qualities within.

Discipline does not impose; it does not control. Discipline guides, teaches and encourages. It's not by accident the words "discipline" and "disciple" come from the same root. Why have disciples followed any great leader, whether you think of Christ, Mohammed, Buddha or any other figure who has earned their place in history? Their disciples follow out of love and respect. Not fear. Discipline gives guidelines, based on respect for each individual. Discipline encourages personal growth.[51]

Think of a parenting situation where the parent takes time to calmly discuss a challenging situation with a child. The parent develops a relationship with the child based on mutual trust. This type of interaction 'ignites' an entirely different part of the brain – the pre-frontal cortex,[52] which is the part of our brain that is able to reason, and process challenging situations, such as being able to see another person's different perspective and predict consequences.

This view of discipline can alter our understanding of self-discipline.

Why Understanding The Difference Between Punishment and Discipline Matters

Talking about discipline is not a deviation from our topic of Wisdom. Our understanding of how God wants to relate to us is going to impact how we are in relationship with Him, and with others. And it's also impacts how we are in relationship with ourselves.

If we see God as One who disciplines, who guides and nurtures and respects our uniqueness, we will recognise a God who won't impose on us but who wants us to develop self-discipline, which is the pathway to using the awesome potential of our brains. When we see God as guiding us because of His immense love for us and His desire for us to grow into more loving, fulfilled human beings, we can respond meaningfully; rather than dropping into "fight" or "flight" reactive behaviours. This is especially important to hold in mind at times when we or our teams are stressed, angry or anxious, because those are the times when we most likely to drop into reactive behaviours. Self-discipline matters most at times when it's hardest to uphold.

When we are tuned in to our clear thinking, and able to use the full faculties of our amazing brains, we will be able to perceive possible consequences of our actions and see situations from different perspectives. We will be able to use conversational skills to create co-operative relationships with others and we will be able to collaboratively make wise choices. And following Wisdom means we will choose self-discipline, which means we will choose to create and uphold our own boundaries.

Self-discipline is our choice. Yes, there will be consequences for our choices. Having the discipline to create and work by a business model that is Wisdom-based is going to reap its own reward - its own natural consequences. There are natural spiritual laws just as there are natural physical laws. Just as the law of gravity still applies, whether you are aware of it or not, so spiritual laws apply. Proverbs maps out the discipline of ethical living. It is a blueprint for success.

> *It's not what we do once in a while that shapes our lives,*
> *it's what we do consistently.*
>
> **Tony Robbins**

Time to reflect:

What is your view of God - One who punishes or One who disciplines to encourage your growth?

What challenges or encourages you in this chapter?

So, what helps us to create the discipline we need for business success?

Chapter 31

The Wisdom of Good Work Habits

One of the easiest ways to develop the self-discipline that leads to success is to create helpful habits and consistently follow through. Whatever path we choose, the consequences will show up. Good intentions by themselves won't make the difference between a mediocre business or an outstanding one that works smoothly to create the success you desire.

Solomon puts discipline alongside Wisdom, in the first couple of verses of Proverbs.

> *The proverbs of Solomon, son of David, king of Israel:*
> *for gaining wisdom and discipline;*
> *for understanding words of insight;*

Proverbs 1:1,2

I know self-discipline is an area that challenges me in my work. Yeah, creative people tend to be messy, but until recently the chaos of my desk was beyond a joke. My workspace wasn't professional. Papers stuck out of my in-tray at all odd angles, submerging my daily diary. My out-tray was a cluster of more papers - but none of them were at the "out" stage. One day I stopped and assessed. My laptop swam in a sea of unsorted paperwork, a cup of yesterday's tea, a tinsel covered headband and four nut-crackers. I was wasting time looking for things. The mess was causing me anxiety as well as stress. I couldn't find what I needed.

Clutter costs time - looking for things that should be accessible. I wasn't checking my priorities and dealing with the most important first because I couldn't see what my priorities were! The clutter was demotivating. *Where do I start!* And I realised one of the reasons I have clutter is because I don't follow a job through until it's done. That means there were remnants of unfinished tasks lying around that had to be returned to. Somehow the pile of clutter on my desk attracted and grew more clutter! I needed to develop the habit of consistently following the job through to completion before starting the next task.

> *they will eat the fruit of their ways...*
>
> Proverbs 1:31a

I reflect on the fruit of my ways in other aspects of my life. I think of how easily I evade taking a regular day off to put work projects entirely aside; that, ultimately, I will not be able to give my best to my work because I have not regularly re-charged my batteries.

Consider the long-term, cumulative impact of our choices regarding our work habits. If we're serious about being successful, we need to be organised and consistent in our habits. This makes the everyday choices easy - nutrition, exercise, relationships, creating attractive, organised space, and how we spend our time. How will we know what's needed to develop helpful daily habits? Wisdom!

If I take a serious look at my work habits, there are aspects of my life where I would still use words like:

~ disorganised

~ cluttered

~ no clear focus.

And if I take a long term, objective view of the "fruit" - the likely outcomes - of those behaviours are:

~ chaos

~ lack of progress

~ poverty mindset and results.

So, in this year ahead I choose to:

~ be disciplined

~ focus on the things that matter most

~ consistently take every task through to completion before moving on to the next

~ be prudent: act with care and thought for the future

~ get back in the saddle as quickly as possible when I slip, without self-flagellation (new habits take time to become embedded).

Any area in your life that has inconsistent results is an area where you have not made a decision to be consistent in your actions.

Jeanine Blackwell

Time to reflect:

If somebody were to observe you in your everyday living, including your work, what might they notice?

What "fruit" would you like to develop in your life?

What habits would you need to develop, or improve, to the outcomes you desire?

Let's take a quick review and then, in the next section, we'll look at what else is essential to create a successful business.

Chapter 32

Going for Gold

Imagine Christopher Columbus as an old man - an astute adventurer from an earlier era than that of Indiana Jones. He took the challenge and discovered a whole new world. He saw things no-one from the western world had ever seen before. It makes sense that he would have experienced fear of the unknown, as well as the fear of mutiny, as crew members began to doubt that they would reach their planned destination. He may well have been concerned that they might run out of resources, but, in considering what he achieved, I imagine he held on to a belief that it was possible to achieve the seemingly impossible.

Likewise, Indiana didn't allow himself to be swayed from his ultimate goal, even though there were challenges to overcome.

Solomon also lived life to the full. His financial wealth gave him the freedom to visit amazing places, pursue things that interested him, meet intriguing people, to live out his dreams - and to make his life count. And he was open in acknowledging that God guided his life.

Commit to the LORD whatever you do,
and he will establish your plans.

Proverbs 16:3

Kings 3:1-28 tells the story of the early stages of the career of Solomon, one of the wealthiest men the world has known. I imagine his journey to success began with a sense of overwhelm and trepidation. We are not given specific details of major upsets Solomon experienced but with the level of leadership he held, we can be sure that challenges arose. But he sought God's guidance as he tried to do the right thing.

Similarly, we know things didn't always go smoothly for Christopher Columbus or for Indiana Jones.

Likewise, when we dare to dream our dreams, take on the responsibilities of leadership in business, and believe for greater things, we *will* face challenges. In this section we've looked at some of the practicalities we may need to address, including:

~ how to ensure anxiety doesn't control your life

~ the importance of the company we keep

~ keeping balance in life

~ how to power through procrastination

~ seeing failure as an essential learning experience, not a brick wall

~ how discipline can help keep us moving forward, especially when we need it the most

~ the power of consistent effective habits to create the transformation we desire.

Having these aspects in place is equivalent to Indiana being able to recognise key markers on the treasure map. However, **if he did not have a compass to head him in the right direction, the map would be of little value.** So, as business people, where can we find our compass for our life journey?

Your Inner Journey as Successful Business Person

Chapter 33

Beliefs - a Different Perspective

Success starts, as Indiana Jones movies do, with the regular person, in their day-to-day life.

When I'm taking "down-time" in my regular life I love doing Wasgijs. What's a Wasgij? The clue is in the word. Read it backwards. Basically, it's a back-to-front jigsaw. When you build a Wasgij you aren't building the picture you can see on the box. You are building what the characters in the picture can see. You have to imagine a totally different perspective. To a great extent you are working with the unknown and the big picture unfolds as you figure out how the pieces fit together. And sometimes you think you have part of the picture sorted only to realise you need to stop and reconfigure the pieces to fit into the bigger scheme of things.

That analogy illustrates a powerful mindset needed to create a successful business. Just like we would do if we were building a Wasgij, we have to look at where we are now, to build a picture that isn't yet apparent. We start with our passion. **We trust there is a big picture - even though we cannot perceive it yet; a divine plan will unfold as we seek Wisdom.**

... those who trust in the Lord will prosper.

Proverbs 28:25b

Our organisation, and our life, is impacted by our beliefs - the stories we tell ourselves that we believe are true. Looking at life through distorted beliefs is like looking at the Wasjig pieces with someone else's reading glasses that mess up our focus. Like the unhelpful message I had previously held that being rich was "filthy", there may be distorted beliefs that blur your vision of the life and business you desire:

"I will never be able to …"

"It's impossible …"

Perhaps these thoughts are most disempowering when you are haunted with images that you are not good enough and that you don't have what it takes; and when you listen to the lies:

"People like me don't succeed."

Often when things will not resolve, there is an underlying belief by which we are still living - so deeply buried we may not recognise it's there. But it's impacting everything we do.

"I thought I had things sorted, but things aren't panning out like I imagined. What's going wrong? I'm putting in the work but the pay-off isn't there!"

What's blocking our progress?

Do you remember as a child holding a sheet of coloured cellophane paper in front of your eyes, and the whole world changed to that colour? Holding the blue, red, or yellow paper in front of our eyes created an alternate world. The colour filter changed our vision and we saw the world differently. In the same way, our beliefs filter our experience of life. And a distorted filter blurs our vision. When we spot the deceptive filter, we can replace the crippling belief with a clearer view of life that will serve us better.

"I can learn what I need to know."

"Anything is possible."

"I can succeed when I'm open to learning and willing to put in the hard work."

It's not our circumstances that trip us up; it's our underlying beliefs that blur our vision that cause us to stumble, making it hard to progress. If we believe we are trapped, we will stay stuck, if we believe we can overcome a challenge, we will find a way. Re-examining our beliefs helps us to see our work from a new, more constructive perspective.

We do not learn from experience. We learn from reflecting on experience.

John Dewey

Time to reflect:

Observe the different pieces of your business and your life:

What is getting in the way of creating the life and business you want?

What might be missing?

What needs rearranging?

What else do you notice?

What difference could that make to your business and to your life?

Inevitably there will be ups and downs in every business. So, what's needed when things get tough?

Chapter 34

When the Going Gets Tough

Being an entrepreneur isn't easy. The adventure feels like fun when we start but it can soon become a never-ending daily - and nightly! - slog. Things can be tough; juggling home and business. Trying to learn so take on board such vast quantities of new information that we don't know where to begin, and the gnawing question of "Will I make it through?" can overwhelm. The business pressures can feel as though they are obstacles to being the person we want to be. But, as Mary O'Malley states, what's in the way IS the way.[53] Apparent obstacles are lessons in themselves. When we are guided by Wisdom, the challenges we face will "burn off" those egocentric parts of our character that get in the way of us being our best selves.

> *The crucible for silver and the furnace for gold,*
> *but the Lord tests the heart.*
>
> Proverbs 17:3

What we need to remember is that **it is not just what we do - but why we do it.** Remembering *why* we initially felt so passionately about our business venture will inspire us to keep going when the going is tough.

If we are in business just for the money or for the ego ride, it won't be enough to fuel us through the challenging times. We need to realise it won't always be easy, and we need to have the courage to follow our hearts and live with integrity. When things are going smoothly, it's easy to act the way we desire, but, when things don't go according to plan, we can be tempted to veer away from our best intentions.

One whose heart is corrupt does not prosper;
one whose tongue is perverse falls into trouble.

Proverbs 17:20

If our hearts are in the wrong place, our tongues will be deceitful, and then we *fall* into trouble. It catches us unawares and we tumble into dire consequences before we know what's happening. What's on our hearts comes out of our mouths. Our thoughts impact how we are within ourselves, both physically and emotionally.

[they will] be filled with the fruit of their schemes.

Proverbs 1:31b

We need to be conscious of where we invest our mental energy, because there are inward consequences to our choices, as well as outward ones.

… whoever listens to me [Wisdom] will live in safety
and be at ease, without fear of harm.'

Proverbs 1:33

Are we setting ourselves up for anxiety, stress, dissatisfaction, uncertainty and dis-ease? Or **is Wisdom leading us to inner calm - a sense of relaxation, confidence and certainty?** *All is well with my soul.*

As water reflects the face,
so one's life reflects the heart.

Proverbs 27:19

Your life is not about you; you are about Life.

Richard Rohr

Time to reflect:

What is uppermost on your heart?

Are your thoughts leading you to inner chaos or to calm certainty and life satisfaction?

What helps you to recalibrate, when needed?

What difference could that make to your business and your life?

We've looked at the power of our beliefs, especially when the going gets tough, but what is one of the most powerful things, in both our business and personal lives, that could block our long-term success?

Chapter 35

Dethrone Ego

Rory comes out of the meeting feeling smug. *They can thank me the meeting was so short!* The agenda had hardly been opened when he jumped in with a barrage of facts. He overpowered people with his knowledge. He side-lined the quieter people who wanted to share their concerns, and steamrollered people into making a hasty decision.

Even so, the vote was close. If he hadn't bulldozed the agenda, the committee might have come to a different decision. Rory thought he'd done a great job. He wasn't aware this hasty decision would lead to countless hours of angst, confusion, and revisiting the situation – causing hours of stress and lost time in the future. He jeopardised working relationships, future decisions, and the long-term success of the project. Rory had the knowledge but he didn't have Wisdom. Self-importance drove his behaviour. His ego over-rode sensitivity to other's needs. He was oblivious to the fact that **only when there is trust and mutual respect are people willing to be transparent and to work collaboratively.**

Similarly, we might have the facts and know how to use them - knowledge - but Wisdom is in another league. The thing is, Wisdom is a lady who doesn't bully her way through. If ego wants to dominate, Wisdom quietly and graciously steps aside. Wisdom never wrestles for position, but is always there for those who seek her.

Does that mean Wisdom is a doormat? No. Wisdom knows Truth will ultimately win. Wisdom intuitively senses the place, the space and the timing to find the most helpful way forward. Wisdom is not in a hurry.

As in the old Irish idiom, "The longest way round is the shortest way home." Issues that are complex are seldom dealt with successfully when we try to hurry the process. Wisdom is patient. Wisdom is discerning. But when we allow ego to rule, Wisdom waits patiently. Ego demands its own way, at any cost. Ego never consults Wisdom. **If we desire Wisdom, we need to dethrone ego.**

Characteristics and Behaviours of Ego

The word "ego" may not have been in Solomon's vocabulary, but he describes the characteristics of the person who is driven by ego:

Proud[54]

Arrogant and conceited[55]

Haughty eyes (infers being judgemental)[56]

Delights in own opinions[57]

Contempt for others[58]

The mindset of ego easily leads to the emotional reactions and behaviours that cause conflict. Religion is often bad-mouthed as the incubator of intolerance and close-mindedness. But here's what neuroscientist Andrew Newberg says:

"The enemy is not religion; the enemy is anger, hostility, intolerance, separatism, extreme idealism, and prejudicial fear - be it secular, religious, or political." [59]

When ego is in control bad outcomes happen.

The rich are wise in their own eyes;

Proverbs 28:11a

Ego is focused on self and it disconnects from others and others' needs. It creates an outlook of "us" and "them"[60] rather than seeing we are all journeying together in life. Solomon says that out of pride and arrogance come evil behaviour and "perverse speech".[61] Ultimately, at every level of society, ego leads to conflict. Why? Because all conflict is a protest at the disconnection; ego is all about the "I" and never about the "We".

Let someone else praise you, and not your own mouth;
an outsider, and not your own lips.

Proverbs 27:2

Wisdom Versus Ego

We do not always know what lies before us. Ego boasts about the future. Wisdom, on the other hand, is present in the Now and esteems connection with our values, with others and with God.

Do not boast about tomorrow,
for you do not know what a day may bring.

Proverbs 27:1

The person with Wisdom perseveres, despite the challenges and disappointments.

Better a patient person than a warrior,
one with self-control than one who takes a city.

Proverbs 16:32

Ego will raise its head in all of us at times, and try to seize control. And that can happen when we are successful and praised for what we have accomplished.

The crucible for silver and the furnace for gold,
but people are tested by their praise.

Proverbs 27:21

Ego feeds on praise; it can cause us to please others rather than fulfil our God-given purpose.

Better to be lowly in spirit along with the oppressed
than to share plunder with the proud.

Proverbs 16:19

This is not saying we choose to be one of the oppressed. It's saying it is better to be among, or alongside, the oppressed than to "share plunder".

"Plunder" is "violent and dishonest acquisition of property".[62]

"But I wouldn't act violently towards anyone!" you're saying?

Chambers Dictionary defines it as: "to steal or remove something precious … in a way that does not consider the moral laws".[63]

Have we ever damaged someone else's reputation or self-esteem?

Have we purchased goods that were made by exploited people?

Consider the impact of our business practices on the earth.

When ego is in control, we are likely to plunder - we are likely to ignore the needs of others.

> *The poor plead for mercy,*
> *but the rich answer harshly.*
>
> **Proverbs 18:23**

Solomon uses juxtaposition of the poor and the rich to point out the consequences of being ruled by ego. It is the poor who suffer the most when megalomaniacs rule. Have we, as capitalist societies, become so ego-focused and absorbed in power and consumerism that we have ignored the cries of the poor?

Is there an alternative solution?

Solomon states all of Wisdom's paths are peace.[64] Not some of Wisdom's paths. *All* the paths of Wisdom are peace. Peace within and world peace.

Why? I perceive it is because Wisdom does not cling to ego.

True contemplatives surrender some of their own ego boundaries and identity so that God can see through them, with them, and in them - with a larger pair of eyes. It is quite simply a higher level of seeing; it is deep consciousness.

Richard Rohr[65]

I ponder Rohr's description of a "larger pair of eyes" - perhaps he is inferring that when we drop the blinkers of ego we see a wider perspective; we see the needs around us.

As I typed this heading "Dethrone Ego" I mis-typed - "dethorn ego". Yes, it's time to de-thorn ego - to remove its barbs. Because it's not that ego is wrong - we need a sense of "I" within the "We". A sense of self is essential in the world of business because we need to start with a firm sense of who we are and what we have to offer. The trouble comes when ego takes charge.

And when I looked at "dethorne" I also noticed "dehorn" - a horned bull is a dangerous animal! It's not that ego is bad. Ego gives us a sense of self – but, when ego runs amock, trouble erupts. Handlers use a ring in a bull's nose to control the powerful creature. What's needed to keep ego from causing chaos and destruction? The nose-ring is humility.

Humility Balances Ego

What makes the difference between humility and ego? It's closely tied to our motives.

> *All a person's ways seem pure to them,*
> *but motives are weighed by the LORD.*
>
> **Proverbs 16:2**

The egocentric person ignores anyone else's needs or perspective. Ego focuses on the "I". Wisdom guides us to the "we" - of connecting with others and connecting with eternal values.

> *Those who trust in their riches will fall,*
>
> **Proverbs 11:28a**

Ego can undermine all our good intentions and the potential value of our work. Solomon offers the solution.

When pride comes, then comes disgrace,
but with humility comes wisdom.

Proverbs 11:2

The word "humility" is one we often misunderstand. Being humble does not mean being a doormat. The word comes from the same root as the word "humus". That means "humility" can be equated with life-giving soil. Humility is about the groundedness of knowing who we are, without giving control to ego.

People often seek honour. They want recognition and fame. But they can fall into ego-based tactics to achieve it. They are trying to grow a garden in stones, instead of cultivating their natural potential.

… humility comes before honour.

Proverbs 15:33b

Ironically the people who achieve true honour aren't seeking it. Think Francis of Assisi, Albert Einstein, Mother Teresa, Nelson Mandela and so many iconic leaders in many different fields - they do what they do because of their passion, not for acclaim. People become leaders because others see their passion and want to follow. When passion and humility walk hand in hand, they are in tune with divine Wisdom.

Humility is the fear of the LORD;
its wages are riches and honour and life.

Proverbs 22:4

A little later in the book I will come back to making sense of the expression "fear of the LORD" – because it is easily misunderstood. But notice the promise in this Proverb that the reward of humility is riches and honour. The thing is, these blessings unfold not because of ego-driven desire but as a natural outcome, because humility opens us to the fertile ground of a life that is so much more than the self-centred "I".

Without humility you are unable to learn.

Lazlo Bock

Time to reflect:

Will you lead from Ego or from the humility of Wisdom?

What might Ego be costing you?

What will help you to put Ego aside?

What difference could that make to your business and your life?

But what if the dictates of ego are not your challenge and you view yourself more like a wilted wallflower?

Chapter 36
Ego's Shadow - False Humility

Some people think they are terribly humble. *Oh, I couldn't possibly stand in front of a crowd. I couldn't lead a meeting. I couldn't start a movement.* In that false humility, the "I" is still ruling. It's self-focused! It ignores what we could be giving to others.

An unfriendly person pursues selfish ends;

Proverbs 18:1a

When we are under stress, we're likely to drop into our default position of self-protection, whether that's parading ego or hiding behind a false humility. Either way our focus is on ourselves, rather than transcending ego so that we can think of what will serve our community. When we put self first, at the expense of others, we diminish the level of connection and we erode their sense of trust.

I refer to this as the "shadow" side of ego. And an interesting aspect of that analogy is that when an object is in shadow its colour and vivacity are muted. Wallflowers are not vibrant. False humility is the opposite of true humility because it is not life-giving - it does not nurture growth in others.

Here's the good news to any reader who feels they are not "good enough", "clever enough", or "worthy enough". Wisdom has been there from the very beginning:

… delighting in the human race.

Proverbs 8:31b[66]

Wow. How does this impact your sense of "not good enough" when you realise God delights in you! You are of value. You have something that you alone can uniquely contribute to the world. You are loved.

Have you ever thought about Jesus' example? He never let ego take control. He was humble (grounded), in a way that brought hope, growth and restoration to others. But he never shied away from speaking out. He was always concerned about the "We" and was certain of God's love for all humanity. He lived in his fullness. He made his life count!

And the day came when the risk to remain tight in bud was more painful than the risk it took to blossom.

Attributed to Anais Nin[67]

Time to reflect:

At times of stress are you are more likely to fall into a default of egoic behaviour or false humility?

What might the shadow side of ego be costing you?

What will help you to step away from your default position and choose Wisdom?

What difference could that make to your business and your life?

So, how to seek Wisdom's guidance to making our lives count?

Chapter 37

Can Our Gut-Feeling Lead to Wisdom?

Does Proverbs encourage us to listen to our gut? In writing this book, I had been working from Proverbs as my base to discover business principles, but here was a question that intrigued me. I couldn't spot that line of thought in Proverbs, but I knew neuroscience has indicated a connection between gut and Wisdom. Our brain isn't only within our heads!

I had an interesting conversation on this topic with business entrepreneur Amanda Delaney, founder of "We Can and We Will" – Ireland. And here's the angle Amanda proposed that was fresh to my thinking.

Our gut aligns with our values. When we sense something is out of kilter - when we have shifted from our "true North", or we are in danger of doing so - we get that uneasy gut feeling.

"Here's the thing," says Amanda. "Most of us are unaware that there is link between our gut and our values. Sometimes we get that unsettled feeling, or the quick lurch, and we don't give it any more attention than maybe thinking we have a bout of wind. We don't slow down enough to listen to our bodies."

The conversation intrigues. What if we were more in tune with our gut feelings? "Everyone chooses different values," shares Amanda. "But we don't make the connection between our values and our gut feeling. What would we gain if we were more aware of this and more aware of the values that uniquely drive us?"

She recommends reading *The Values Factor: The Secrets to Creating and Inspiring a Fulfilling Life* by Dr John F. Demartini.

My mind buzzes because I know that Proverbs is big into values. What if we tune in to our gut reaction - will it guide us to the True North of our values? I return to Proverbs to see what I can excavate. But it eludes me. I can't find anything in Proverbs about gut. It's some days later I'm pondering this when my thoughts turn to the Proverb that describes lazy people as being like "vinegar to the teeth".[68] I let my mind focus on the sensation of vinegar on the teeth. *Oooh, the edginess.* My salivation increases. My lips draw back. I inadvertently swallow. *My stomach has knotted!* Even imagining vinegar in my mouth causes a somatic reaction.

My body knows when something is not right - it has to be in Proverbs! What am I overlooking? Okay the word "gut" isn't there. What other word would Solomon use? Belly or stomach!

From the fruit of their mouth a person's stomach is filled;
with the harvest of their lips they are satisfied.
Proverbs 18:20

Here's the link between our gut and values. Our words express our values - and they satisfy us, and our gut signals when we are aligned with True North.

Can our strong emotions give a distorted gut message? Can they cause a "magnetic field" that confuses our True North? Yes. But that doesn't mean the inner compass isn't working. The signal is there, and to recognise it we need to be attuned to our inner knowing. Our gut feel can be Wisdom's guidance to making our lives count. **Sometimes that tug in our stomach is a signal we need to close the gap between our behaviour and our values.**

We'll delve deeper into that a little later in the book.

When what you value and dream about doesn't match the life you are living, you have pain.

Shannon L. Alder

Time to reflect:

Think of a time when your gut was giving you a message.

Did you heed it - or not?

What was the outcome?

What would help you to tune in to your body's inner knowing?

What difference could that make to your business and to your life?

So, what will help us to stay in tune with our values?

Chapter 38

When a Leader Compromises Their Integrity

I had been reading the fifth chapter of Proverbs. Solomon referred to adultery two chapters earlier and now here was a whole chapter on the same topic.[69]

You may be thinking: "I'm not committing adultery. Shall I skip this chapter?"

Wait a moment! What if there's a deeper and more profound message here? What's so important about this topic that it's given such high profile? Can adultery be a metaphor when used in the context of applying Wisdom to business?

Why was this topic such a mega-deal to Solomon? I ponder his background. Aha! The clues begin to align. King David is his father. David - the philanderer who fancied the beautiful woman bathing on the rooftop. More than a powerful king can resist; he sends for her.

His supreme power means he gets his way with her. But he gets more than he anticipates when she tells him she's pregnant with his child. This is going to be a problem, even for a king. Bathsheba's husband is one of his best generals - away leading his men in battle - winning the war for his king. His wife in the family way! Not exactly an easy problem to explain away.

Get the man home. He'll think it's his child, if he doesn't do the sums too carefully!

But even when David invites Uriah to the palace and plies him with alcohol, he refuses to go home and sleep with his wife while his men are out there in the trenches.

This isn't working. I've got to get rid of this guy. Before he finds out the truth!

Oh, what a web we weave, when at first we deceive.

Shakespeare

I imagine Solomon growing up in the royal household. His father is the king - the coolest, most powerful dude in the whole land! Until…! Maybe Solomon is in his teens when he hears whispered taunts:

"You think your dad's so great! If only you knew!"

"What are they saying!"

Solomon begins to ask questions. He discovers his dad's adultery and his attempted cover-ups.

"My dad murdered my mother's first husband! And he was one of the king's most loyal generals! My dad deliberately had him killed on the frontline of the battlefield!"

Solomon's worldview must have come crashing down around him. No wonder he wanted to get his point across that adultery was never okay! Adultery isn't a fashionable word. Call it an affair, call it a fling - it's still the same thing because it smashes and shatters lives.

Honesty is the first chapter in the book of wisdom.

Thomas Jefferson

Maybe you have been stung by adultery, or maybe not - but what is the deeper message which applies to all of us?

Adultery isn't as much about who you lie with - it's who you lie to.

Harriet Lerner

Commitment and honesty matter. You can't have an affair without falling into the trap of lying. Lying to the person you committed to. Deceiving your family. Deceiving colleagues. Trying to lie to God that this is okay. And lying to the person you see in the mirror. Deceiving your own values. Pretending this is okay when you know it isn't.

What this means is that adultery erodes your integrity. And without integrity we are not following Wisdom. We can read the whole chapter of Proverbs 5 as a warning to guard our integrity - a challenge to be the person we want to be.

> *for an adulterous woman is a deep pit …*
> *Like a bandit she lies in wait …*
>
> **Proverbs 23:27a, 28a**

This is someone who takes what is not rightfully theirs. It's interesting that this a topic Proverbs returns to time and again. In biblical literature, repetition is a signal: the message is important!

Proverbs 6:27 compares adultery to scooping fire in your lap or walking on hot coals. It's going to leave you in pain and permanently damaged.

PeopleSpeak: Don't play with fire!

Perennial success will develop when we live by a code of integrity - what's going on inside us is congruent with our outer actions. Our words will reflect what is within. Being the business-person we desire to be is only going to happen if we have done the inner housecleaning. We need to sweep out the dirt, clear the clutter and set things in order.

> *The words of the mouth are deep waters,*
>
> **Proverbs 18:4a**

Integrity is not an add-on optional extra. And when integrity guides our decisions, we will like the person we see in the mirror.

> *We hurt ourselves when we give our time, the minutes of our lifespan,*
> *to pursuits that don't match our own values.*
>
> Anne Katherine

> **Time to reflect:**
>
> What business seductions could lure you off course:
>
> Money? Public acknowledgement? Sexual attraction? Power?
>
> What is the Wisdom you need today, whatever you may be facing inwardly or outwardly?
>
> What difference could that make to your business and to your life?

Integrity is key. And integrity makes us people who do the right thing. But how do we know what we need to know to do the right thing?

Chapter 39

Seek Knowledge and Understanding

W̲e all know enthusiasts who have great ideas but don't put them into action.

Fools find no pleasure in understanding
but delight in airing their own opinions.

Proverbs 18:2

It's not going to help if you have zeal (energy and enthusiasm to achieve your goal) if you don't have knowledge (the facts, information, skills and practical understanding to make it happen).

... the one who cherishes understanding will soon prosper.

Proverbs 19:8b

To prosper is to do well, to grow strong and healthy. It infers financial success. We can have the knowledge - the facts and information - but if we don't apply it, it is no more than facts in our heads. **Knowledge in itself, without application, will not cause us to prosper.**

163

I'm a great reader but I know one of my weaknesses is that I read books and think, "That's important!" but carry on to the next chapter or the next book, without putting into action what I've learnt.

Like the useless legs of one who is lame
is a proverb in the mouth of a fool.

Proverbs 26:7

PeopleSpeak: All talk and no action.

Take time to gain the knowledge, then figure out why this matters: what this means for your business and how you are going to implement it. Create a plan of action.

To read without reflecting is like eating without digesting.

Edmond Burke

Time to reflect:

On a scale of 1 - 10 are you consuming information without digesting it?

What would help you improve your "digestion" of knowledge?

What one small doable step can you take this week to support you in "digesting" knowledge.

How will you record your progress?

What difference could that make to your business and your life?

Let's take a quick recap of these reflections of our inner journey.

Chapter 40
Going for Gold

If you know the Indiana Jones series, you need only to see a silhouette of actor Harrison Ford in this role to recognise the iconic stance of Indiana. His confidence and determination are evident – the erect stature, legs strongly grounded, arms ready to for action. Indiana's character resonates with us because we sense his integrity, his courage to stand for justice and for those who matter to him. We sense he holds to his values, and believes in his ability to overcome the challenges he faces.

Here are some of the key thoughts from this section, that help us to read the compass - to follow the true North for our life journey.

As we have discussed, there are inwards challenges, as well as outward ones that entrepreneurs face. **Our business, and life, is impacted by our beliefs - the stories we tell ourselves that we believe are true.** There may be thoughts that aren't helping to build the life and business we desire. These thoughts are most destructive when we are haunted with images that we are not good enough, that we don't have what it takes; when we listen to the lie that people like us don't succeed. But the challenge is that the more we listen to the stories we tell ourselves, the more we believe them.

Often when situations will not resolve, there's an underlying belief we are still living by - so deeply buried we don't recognise it is there but it is impacting everything we do. The good news is, when we recognise the distorted belief, we can refocus!

Are our thought patterns leading us to anxiety, stress, dissatisfaction, uncertainty and dis-ease? Or is Wisdom leading us to inner calm - a sense of relaxation, confidence and certainty?

If we desire Wisdom, we need to dethrone ego. Ego demands its own way at any cost. It never consults Wisdom. The mindset of ego can easily lead to conflict, because ego is all about self and it disconnects from others and other's needs.

We also looked at false humility: the "I" is still ruling. It's self-focused, even if it is a wallflower! If we want peace - within ourselves, within our communities and at a global level - we need to let go of ego and look to Wisdom.

We reflected on how our gut-feel can lead us to Wisdom, because it signals when we are not aligned with our values. Living by our values is the essence of integrity, and when integrity guides our decisions, we will like the person we see in the mirror. We need to realign with our true North.

Whoever gives heed to instruction prospers,

Proverbs 16:20a

We have recognised that knowledge in itself will not cause us to prosper. **Knowing the relevant facts is vital for business success, but knowledge has an expiry date. Wisdom always holds true.**

Sometimes we've shaken out unhelpful beliefs and applied the knowledge and understanding, but things still don't seem to be headed in the right direction. Let's turn to the next section to discover why Wisdom makes such a powerful difference in relationships.

SECTION G

The Awesome Treasure of IQ, EQ and More

Chapter 41

The Essential Keys to Relationship Success

W e've all heard of hugely successful business people like Sir Richard Branson who didn't shine at school. They didn't achieve the required academic results in the formal system of education. But they went on to shine in their own glorious way.

Since the early 1900s IQ tests have been used to measure intelligence; deciding who - according to that standard - is bright and who is supposedly not so bright. This emphasis on IQ dominated the Western world's schooling system in the 1900s and still confines the unique potential of people who don't "fit the box".

Nearly eighty years later Howard Gardner introduced the theory of multiple intelligences[70] - that different people are gifted in different ways. Soon emotional intelligence[71] shared the stage. It is now recognised that cognitive intelligence alone is not enough for success. Business success requires the soft skills of social intelligence - the ability to interact well with others.

And now there are new kids on the block - conversational intelligence[72] and relational intelligence.[73]Actually, they have been there all the time — we just hadn't put those names on them; and our society is now recognising their value. When we have well-honed conversational skills, we know how to connect with people, how to hear their dreams and vulnerabilities, and share our own. Success does not depend only on how smart we are, but how we use relational skills to build trust and collaboration. In my reading of the Proverbs, I perceive that Solomon was aware of the power of these "intelligences" - millennia before they became officially recognised as significant factors in leadership. No success story has ever been "I did it by myself!" Even if your work crew are your family, friends and virtual assistants, success relies upon your relational skills as leader to create team collaboration.

Why Trust Is Essential for Positive Interactions

Conversational skill isn't based merely on logical thinking. Its essence is Wisdom and it builds relationships of mutual confidence and trust. Trust isn't a given. In any relationship trust fluctuates because our mood, our energy levels and behaviours fluctuate. Each of us see things from a different perspective and we have differences of opinion. We won't always be in synchronicity with one another. When disparities happen, it leads to disconnection, which leads to conflict. Rupture and repair happen in every relationship. It's how we deal with it that counts. We need honesty, transparency and social and emotional intelligence to build trust. These, together with deep listening skills, are the essence of relationship. Solomon might not have used this terminology but he understood the concepts.

Hold a non-judgemental attitude.

Whoever derides their neighbour has no sense.

Proverbs 11:12a

Nothing erodes trust faster than a critical spirit.

Respect confidentiality.

A key factor of conversational skill is that you can be trusted not to share other people's stories without permission:

… the one who has understanding holds their tongue.

Proverbs 11:12b

I do not believe this intends confidentiality at all costs. Crime and abuse must be reported. Solomon was a magistrate, which means that he openly addressed unlawful conduct. He knew that holding clear boundaries in conversation mattered.

Develop your relational skills.

Solomon recognises the link between rich conversation and our inner experience:

> *The tongue of the righteous is choice silver,*
> *but the heart of the wicked is of little value.*

Proverbs 10:20

The message from the tongue is impacted by the attitude of the heart. Conversational skill isn't only about what happens in our heads, it impacts our emotions as well. Consider this metaphor of silver to describe the art of deep listening.

Silver is a precious metal that takes effort to mine from the deep before it is processed to remove impurities. It is of value not only for its beauty but for its strength and functionality. Silver is naturally resistant to corrosion. This precious metal is not a cheap throw-away - it lasts. Throughout history precious metals have been a benchmark of value because they don't deteriorate. Quality conversation is "choice silver".

Are we, as team leaders, listening well so that our teams develop the art of talking well? Are we listening to our clients and customers? **Conversational skill is not a pebble on the beach; it is a rare treasure that takes patience, skill and focus.** Yet, like silver, it can be found, sometimes unexpectedly, in everyday settings! A relationship built on the trust of being able to openly share is pure silver.

Create openness and honesty in conversations.

> *Whoever winks with their eye is plotting perversity;*

Proverbs 16:30a

In other words, the one who is deliberately deceitful is going to cause trouble, catastrophe and suffering.

Here's what might this sound like if we look at it from a positive angle:

Whoever is open and honest is planning for success.

Ensure your conversation contributes to well-being.

> *… a perverse tongue will be silenced.*
>
> **Proverbs 10:31b**

"Perverse" refers to behaviour that is unacceptable or unreasonable. [74] Ultimately, the voice that does not add quality to conversation will not be heard. Being reasonable - the opposite of perversity - is needed to build mutual respect and trust.

Knowing when to talk, when not to talk, and how to deeply listen are key elements to building trust and building a team who dream incredible dreams and make them a reality. Think of tremendous developments which have transformed our world – water on tap, electricity, health care, the personal computer. These have happened because the environment was created for the impossible to become possible. Creating that environment of collaboration takes discernment, care and patience.

Choose patience and practise self-control - *especially* when it's difficult!

> *Better a patient person than a warrior,*
> *one with self-control than one who takes a city.*
>
> **Proverbs 16:32**

The person with self-control always holds clear, consistent boundaries. They will ascertain and uphold what does or doesn't belong in a conversation. Clear limits are like the walls of a city: they are established to safeguard those within.

Other Gems about Wise Conversation

What else can we learn from Proverbs about conversational skills?

> *Sin [missing the mark] is not ended by multiplying words*
> *but the prudent hold their tongues.*
>
> **Proverbs 10:19**

Peoplespeak: Don't speak unless you have something worth saying.

> *The wise store up knowledge,*
> *but the mouth of a fool invites ruin.*
>
> **Proverbs 10:14**

This proverb is hinting that the wise person is listening! They store up knowledge when they hear what others have to say, taking the information and processing it into knowledge.

> *From the mouth of the righteous comes the fruit of wisdom,*
>
> **Proverbs 10:31a**

Fruit is ready in the right season. It's not just what we say, it's when we say it.

> *A person finds joy in giving an apt reply –*
> *and how good is a timely word!*
>
> **Proverbs 15:23**

The wise leader consciously encourages meaningful conversation.

> *… gracious words promote instruction.*
>
> **Proverbs 16:21b**

When we are in tune with divine Wisdom, we'll find the "proper answer" (Proverbs 16:1) and we will promote collaborative learning. We will know what to say, and how and when to say it.

Gracious words are a honeycomb,
sweet to the soul and healing to the bones.

Proverbs 16:24

Imagine living in earlier times when processed sugar wasn't part of the diet. Honeycomb must have been the sweetest thing imaginable, and honey has natural healing properties. Likewise, Proverbs 10:21a says the lips of the righteous nourish many. Relational skills can heal conflicts and build trust.

Deep trust is the ultimate currency.

Sam Conniff Allende

Time to reflect:

What verse or thought in this chapter most challenges you?

Do your words bring healing, relief and sweetness to others' lives?

Does your conversation empower and enrich other people, both online and offline?

What aspect of your conversational skills need honing?

What will support you to strengthen your conversational skill?

What difference could that make to your business and to your life?

We've focused in this chapter on the art of wise conversation. What specific advice does Solomon give regarding talking wisely?

Chapter 42

Talking Wisely

Solomon obviously developed the art of talking wisely. Much of his focus on this topic is regarding the habits of those who have not given attention to how they speak.

Solomon's Advice on How to Avoid Talking Foolishly

Let's consider his comments regarding negative interaction and then infer what the opposite of that behaviour might be.

Careless Talk:

> *The mouths of fools are their undoing,*
>
> Proverbs 18:7a

I reflected on "undoing".[75]

We could say, from the mouths of fools - those who lack moral guidance – come words that are:

- their Achilles heel

- their downfall

- their collapse

- their failure

- their affliction

- their destruction

- their defeat.

If those are the outcomes of foolish words, what are the outcome of wise words? Here are opposites of "undoing".[76]Wise words will give:

- advantage

- fortune

- honour

- prosperity

- respect

- success

- triumph

- strength

- benefit

- blessing

- building up

- comfort

- contentment.

Aren't these the qualities we desire for our business? And our lives!

Divisive Talk:

The lips of fools bring them strife,
and their mouths invite a beating.

Proverbs 18:6

Unwise words can bring a beating – **perhaps not literally, but this could infer a financial 'beating'**. If the lips of the fool bring strife, then it makes sense the lips of the wise can bring calm and harmony.

Insincere Talk:

> *Like a coating of silver dross on earthenware*
> *are fervent [smooth] lips with an evil heart.*
>
> **Proverbs 26:23**

Dross is the scum from the metal-making process - it's not the real thing. The person who deceives can speak with such smooth talk that, at first, we are taken in by words spoken with a passionate intensity but, over time, the "silver dross" will chip or flake off to reveal the true nature.

We need to ensure we speak sincerely.

Deceitful Talk:

> *A lying tongue hates those it hurts,*
> *and a flattering mouth works ruin.*
>
> **Proverbs 26:28**

Devious words can damage those they target and can cause pain. And they can also boomerang.

> *… their lips are a snare to their very lives.*
>
> **Proverbs 18:7b**

I ponder the word "snare". A snare is a deception – a serious danger that wasn't apparent until it was too late. How often do foolish words trap a person in an awkward situation!

So, to reflect on the opposite of a snare, honest words can bring:

- freedom

- liberation

- frankness (without deception).

Malevolent Talk:

> *The words of a gossip are like choice morsels;*
> *they go down to the inmost parts.*
>
> **Proverbs 18:8**[77]

Gossip is sharing what is not ours to share — it is slander and defamation of character. These words go down to our innermost parts - we digest and assimilate them. Just as eating unhealthy food has an impact on our well-being, so too does ingesting degrading words make us unwell. The bottom line - don't consume or regurgitate gossip!

So, we might consider the opposite of spreading gossip is giving encouragement and commenting on what we appreciate about others. Similarly, the opposite of the deception could be seen as talking with transparency and openness. Let's deal with facts we can substantiate - not letting our imaginations create stories that could cause defamation of character. **When we are wise, we use words not to break, but to affirm and encourage.**

Derisive Talk:

> … people detest a mocker.
>
> **Proverbs 24:9b**

Mocking is a form of bullying. Our words break others down or build them up. People will judge our character by our words.

Perversive Talk:

> *Better the poor whose way of life is blameless*
> *than a fool whose lips are perverse.*

Proverbs 19:11

Perverse is defined as unreasonable, uncooperative, unaccommodating and annoying.[78]

In other words, be reasonable, cooperative, accommodating.

And let your talk not be annoying. The opposite of annoying would be to let your talk be:

composed, assured, steady, uplifting, relaxed, conciliatory, soothing, defusing, agreeable, supportive, cheering, enchanting, animated. [79]

Rather than talking in a manner that deliberately undermines or consumes the space, choose to talk in a manner that creates connection.

Considering all these aspects, the quality of our talk is important to create the business success we desire.

Solomon's Advice on How to Talk Wisely

Know When to Keep Quiet

Perhaps the beginning of wise talking is learning what not to say. Graciously holding silence is a discipline. We need to test our intention: "Is this helpful?" before we engage our tongues. **Part of wise talking is being careful what conversations we choose to open up, and the ones from which to step away.**

> *Even fools are thought wise if they keep silent,*
> *and discerning if they hold their tongues.*

Proverbs 17:28

Do not answer a fool according to his folly,
or you yourself will be just like him.

Proverbs 26:4

Affirm and Encourage

From the fruit of their mouth a person's stomach is filled;
with the harvest of their lips they are satisfied.
The tongue has the power of life and death,
and those who love it will eat its fruit.

Proverbs 18:20, 21

Words that build will return blessing. Words of ridicule or aggression, sexism, racism or other slurs sow seeds of discord that grow to entangle and choke out the good. This principle applies not only to individuals but to communities. When we use our tongues in ways that demean and demoralise, it will come back to haunt us.

"The tongue has the power of life and death" is a challenging thought. The words we say are never neutral; they are either words that lead to life or words that lead to death. There is a harvest that will come to fruition - weeds or life-giving crops, depending on the seeds we sow. When we recognise the power of our words and the harvest we create, we will choose to talk more wisely.

Your Words Reveal Your Character

The words of the mouth are deep waters,

Proverbs 18:4a

We use the expression "off the top of my head" but even a few words can reveal the depths of our hearts. The words we use are indicative of our inner journey.

Recognise the Power of your Words

Proverbs 25:11[80], in the Good News translation, describes a well-articulated idea as being like "a design of gold, set in silver." Our words can be valuable - inspiring and motivating to others.

> *One… who speaks with grace*
> *will have the king for a friend.*
>
> **Proverbs 22:11b**

When we learn the art of speaking wisely, people of influence will trust us and appreciate us.

Take Particular Care in the Relationships that Matter Most

> *He who finds a wife finds what is good*
> *and receives favour from the Lord.*
>
> **Proverbs 18:22**

Perhaps, it is in our most intimate relationships, that the tongue will reap the greatest harvest. Perhaps this is where we have the greatest challenge - it's the space where we can most easily fall into criticism, control and negativity. And our homes are where we most need to give and receive words that encourage. It's the space where we most need connection and harmony. We will bear the fruit of our words, especially in our intimate relationships.

Try as we might, none of us is able to compartmentalise personal life from work. Work stresses can contaminate home space, unless we are vigilant. Conversely, when home relationships are happy and satisfying, then that positive energy is likely to flow through into our work space.

> *Through patience a ruler can be persuaded,*
> *and a gentle tongue can break a bone.*
>
> **Proverbs 25:15**

A situation that seemed as permanent and inflexible as bone can be altered when we speak wisely. People listen not only to our words but to our tone. They sense our attitude and our mood. It's not just what we say, it's how and when we say it.

Business, like life, is all about how you make people feel. It's that simple,
and it's that hard.

Danny Meyer

Time to reflect:

What does "speaking with grace" mean to you?

Who do you admire because of their skill in speaking with grace?

How would others describe your talking habits?

Which verse in this chapter most challenges you?

What do you choose to do about that?

What difference could that make to your business and to your life?

Alongside developing the art of talking well, how do we develop the art of listening wisely?

Chapter 43
Listening Wisely

I tried to explain to the shop floor manager that this item, purchased from their store, was a gift to me. Here's my half of the conversation and I'll leave it to your imagination to fill in the rest.

"It's not what I need and I can't see another item in the store that I'd like. Please may I have a refund."

…

"No. I don't have the credit card that was used for the purchase. This was a gift to me."

…

"So, you won't give me a refund?"

…

"I've already looked. No - I can't find anything else I'd like."

…

"You're suggesting I look upstairs to find a pretty dress to buy."

Are you saying my dress isn't pretty!

It's strange how an incident can stay in your head years later. The floor manager's intransigence meant I eventually chose a replacement item - *not* a dress! She stuck rigidly to "shop policy" and made no effort to collaboratively find a way forward. She imposed her solution. She didn't listen to what my needs were. She won the battle but lost the war. I never shopped in her shop again.

Why Business People Need to Develop the Art of Listening Well

One of the greatest skills and personal assets a business-person can develop is to listen well. To listen deeply means people feel understood, and when they feel understood they feel connected, which means conflict naturally dissolves. This makes sense because **all conflict is a protest at the disconnection**, which defuses when we feel connected. The disconnection is likely to be between the persons concerned, but there may also be other disconnections - such as a disconnection from important information that would influence thinking, or an inner conflict may be owing to a disconnection from one's own values. **Listening well can build bridges so that disconnections are resolved.**

When we develop the skill of listening, we connect with our team and our customers; they will tell us more about what matters to them. We can respond to what they need. And this means we gain loyal clients who want to tell others about their positive experiences with our brand. Listening well is also a key to developing a motivated team who collaborate well and who create innovative solutions.

In this chapter and the next, let's look at a few more verses in Proverbs 18 to discover the art of listening wisely. At first glance, verses 13-17 seem to jump from one disparate thought to another, but what if we view each of these five verses in Proverbs through the lens of listening? Let's reflect on some of these verses here – and then return to this passage in the following chapter, where we look at how to listen well.

Listening Well Supports Well-being

The human spirit can endure in times of illness,
but a crushed spirit who can bear?

Proverbs 18:14

Listening well means we support others' emotional well-being. The key to restoring a person's spirit is for them to experience being deeply listened to — listened to in a way that helps them to remember who they are, what truly matters, and what their purpose is in life. People can journey through tough times if their spirits are strong. In my favourite theatre production *Lion King*, Simba, whose spirit has been crushed, is reminded, "Remember who you are."

"Re-membering" is picking up the broken pieces and putting the members (pieces) back together again. When we listen deeply, we help people to "re-member" who they are. They remember they are called to be whole - to live as children of God. **When listened to wisely, restoring of the person's crushed spirit is possible.** The good news is that wise listening is a skill any person can gain. We can listen in a way that supports the person to revive their drooping self-esteem, to pick up their crushed spirit and find meaning and purpose again.

Listen to Other Viewpoints

When we hold an enquiring mindset to hear other viewpoints - from our advisers, from our team-members, from those who love us, from our clients or customers - we get to see and respond to different perspectives. We can listen with compassionate curiosity.

When we listen well, we support people to consider different aspects of a situation they may not have seen before. The more angles we have on a scenario the more we gain a sense of the context. The more we can see the big picture and understand a situation, the clearer we become on what we don't know, and what we need to know and discern.

> *In a lawsuit the first to speak seems right,*
> *until someone comes forward and cross-examines.*
>
> **Proverbs 18:17**

We can discover more about a situation by listening to different perspectives, and the more we will learn, the clearer picture we will have of what we do know, what we don't know, what our options are, and what's needed. This means we can determine the core question that needs answering, that will give insight into the way forward!

At times, deep listening reveals such profound thinking we sense the working of God:

A gift opens the way
and ushers the giver into the presence of the great.

Proverbs 18:16

Develop the art of listening to deeply hear the other. This matters because when we create a safe space which helps the other person to hear themselves think it not only restores the person's sense of self, it is often what's needed for fresh ideas to rise to the surface. **Sometimes, as leaders, it's not so much about our own ideas or knowledge but about wise listening.** And when we model active listening our team members are likely to absorb this approach.

Create the space for your team to interact more collaboratively to find the fresh solutions that could have ground-breaking results. Wise listening leads to connection and collaboration, which means your team has a sense of "buy in". When people experience being part of the solution they contribute more and commit themselves to the success of the project.

Listening Is a Gift We Give Others

Think back to the situation I shared about the shop floor manager. Store policy might have not have made it possible for her to offer a solution, but if she had listened empathetically, I would have felt heard. Very often, that, in itself, is enough to create a different, mutually respectful outcome.

When we listen with compassionate curiosity and empathy, we offer healing to people's spirits and souls. And wise listening is not passive. It is active and engaged. Skilled listeners build rapport – they are tuned in to the other person's experience. When we aren't sensitive and responding to the other person's experience, such as when a listener responds in an upbeat manner when a person is grieving, it creates a dissonance that can be experienced as painful by the other person.

Like one who takes away a garment on a cold day,
or like vinegar poured on a wound,
is one who sings songs to a heavy heart.

Proverbs 25:20

When we hold a non-judgmental, empathic listening space, people sense it and speak freely. With deep listening, we can open the recesses into people's hearts and to the thoughts they didn't yet know they were thinking. **There is a potential greatness within each one of us that lies dormant until it is brought into the light.**

In the NIVUK Bible there is a footnote suggesting this alternative translation:

As water reflects the face,
so others reflect your heart back to you.

Proverbs 27:19

The wise listener is able to reflect not only the other person's thoughts but how they feel about the issue they are discussing. The listener enables the person to "feel felt" - that somebody truly gets what they are trying to convey. Not only at head level but at heart level - the listener senses and responds to the person's shared frustration, passion or whatever emotion is driving the conversation. And when there are secure boundaries of things told in trust and the person feels understood, they will sense it's a safe space to share.

Listening wisely is probably the greatest gift you can give, to the other person and also to your business.

Dialogue does not only mean listening but being in a constant attitude
of welcoming the gift of the other.

Archbishop Pizzaballa

Time to reflect:

When you feel your spirit is crushed, where is your safe space where you experience being deeply listened to?

When others need to feel heard, how safe a space are you?

What difference could that make to your business and to your life?

So, how to develop the listening skills that can transform your business?

Chapter 44

Developing Super-Power Listening Skills

There is a difference between hearing and listening deeply. For example, you can hear music playing but are you *listening?* Are you tuning in to hear the nuances and emotion of the music; to notice the melody and repeated patterns, the change in tempo, and to be aware of the sound of the different instruments? You won't notice the subtleties and richness of a piece of music unless you give it your full attention and *listen.*

I'm naturally a talker rather than a listener. In my younger days, deep listening was a mystery I couldn't fathom: a treasure I didn't know how to unearth. It seemed as though it was a rare jewel you either had or didn't have. But I discovered deep listening is a skill we can all develop. Here are three key insights about how to listen that can transform our relationships and create amazing business breakthrough.

Don't Interrupt - Stay in "Listen" Mode

> *To answer before listening —*
> *that is folly and shame.*
>
> Proverbs 18:13

We jump in with our answer before we have truly listened. We listen to interrupt. So often we are waiting for the first opportunity to leap in and express our opinion or to correct the other. We put on a semblance of listening while we focus our attention on formulating our reply. **True listening is being fully present to the other person's experience and perception.**

Often, we think we know that the other person is going to say, so we start talking before they have finished their sentence. We need to learn to listen until the other person has said their full stop – has got to the end of what they are saying. If we are attentive, we will hear their "full stop" when they have completed expressing their thought.

To answer before listening is interrupting. And when we interrupt, we don't hear what the other is trying to share. We give a message:

   – What I have to say is more important than what you're saying

   – Your thoughts don't matter

   – What you are experiencing doesn't matter

   – I know better than you.

Perhaps you are thinking, "I don't interrupt!"

Our body language interrupts when we:

- glance at our watch or at our smart phone

- frown or fold our arms

- click our tongue

- roll our eyes

- raise an eyebrow

- shake our heads in disagreement

- draw in our breath ready to speak, whilst the other person is still mid-sentence.

Our body language answers before we have listened and people sense the interruption.

If people don't feel the safety of your listening presence, they won't articulate the thoughts they are trying to formulate. When we interrupt, we shut down their possibility thinking – team members won't be likely to share their creative thoughts that can lead to innovative solutions to business challenges.

When we interrupt we damage their sense of trust. They won't share their vulnerability, their inspiration or their aspirations. We won't develop the quality of relationship that creates motivation and inspiration.

"To answer before listening that is folly."

What if we put the word "folly" under the microscope?[81]

To answer before listening is:

- craziness

- madness

- idiocy

- stupidity

- indiscretion

- recklessness

- imprudence (not thinking about what's beneficial for the long term).

And what if we look at that proverb from a different perspective, by looking at the opposite of "folly".

To listen before answering:

- is intelligent

- is wise

- makes sense

- is using discretion

- is prudent

- requires taking care.

Listening deeply is foundational to building trust in relationship. And we need a foundation of trust to create the quality of conversation that leads to transformative thinking. The key to those breakthrough *"Aha's!"* that take a business from average to exponential are most likely to happen when deep listening is in tandem with incisive questioning. An incisive question is one that cleanly and precisely cuts to the heart of the matter. Every wise entrepreneur knows how to wield powerful questions.

The Power of Questions

Finding the incisive questions to ask is the key to opening the door to fresh solutions that can evoke ground-breaking results. Here's one key tip from life coaching:

Don't use "why?" questions, use "what?" questions.

Apart from the extreme valuable question, *"WHY* does this matter?", which establishes the purpose of your organisation or your project, *"why?"* questions are generally unhelpful, unless you're a scientist.

"Why?" questions often cause backward-looking and give a subtle message of blame. And when people sense they are being blamed they duck under cover, make excuses or try to pass the blame to someone else.

"What?" questions are more helpful. They are forward-looking and solution-focused. They encourage collaboration.

"What could we do differently?"

"What's stopping us?"

"What needs to happen?"

When you sense a *"why?"* question coming into your head, stop, and rephrase it as a *"what?"* question. This is likely to encourage greater responsible, and unearth more innovative thinking, that can lead to more synergistic results.

You can effectively use *"what?"* questions in conversation with your clients, too.

When we receive feedback that is affirming but generalised, *"what"* questions can help us to glean more specific information about our customers' likes or dislikes. This creates the opportunity for us to respond more precisely to what they want and need, which means we can create products that sell.

For instance, here's how I might respond when a client makes a comment,

I love your book!

Thank you. What was it you loved?

The answers to "what" questions can give me helpful insights for my future books!

Likewise, if someone is frank enough to give you negative criticism, see it as a gift to learn more about what your client needs and wants.

I read your book, but there were some aspects I didn't like.

Thank you for your feedback. What was it you didn't like?

(That doesn't mean you let people dump garbage on you!) Responding graciously with "what" questions opens the door to gain feedback that can be the key to transforming your business from mediocre to mega-successful.

There is a caveat to this: don't change your product if you receive a single negative comment. Listen for patterns of consistent feedback from a number of people. Over time you might repeatedly hear feedback that indicates something needs adjusting. But there are also times a person might make one comment that so resonates with your spirit, that you know they have put their finger on something that needs addressing.

"What questions" work fabulously in having problem-solving conversations with yourself!

"What could I do differently?"

"What's stopping me?"

"What is within my control /power to bring the change I need?"

"What's my potential 20 per cent effort that will give 80% leverage?"

If you would like to know more about how to use questions to solve challenging work problems, here is your link to a complimentary copy of one of my key training videos: "How to Open Up Possibility Thinking":

https://koemba.com/solving-sticky-problems

If I had an hour to solve a problem and my life depended on the solution,
I would spend the first 55 minutes determining the proper question to ask...
For once I knew the proper question, I could solve the problem in less than 5 minutes.
Albert Einstein

The Power of "What if?"

"What if" questions are also hugely powerful, both within the team context, and also to develop our own possibility thinking.

"What if ...?" questions take our thinking further than we have taken it before. 'What if ...?" questions support our team to solve the challenges before them, like Indiana Jones deciphering clues so that he can access treasures that had previously been inaccessible to everybody else.

The next time your team face a situation that seems impossible to untangle, try using an open-ended "What if ...?" question.

What I mean by "open-ended", in this context, is a question for which you do not yet know the answer.

Open-ended "What if...?" questions are a powerful precision tool for possibility thinking, creating space for people to open up and explore their unthought thoughts and expand their own understanding. So, here are examples of open-ended "what if..." questions for transformative results:

Your team may be concerned, "We don't have the resources to do this."

Notice what unfolds when you ask,

"What if we did have the resources to do this?"

Your team may be puzzled about a problem:

"We don't know what to do."

"What if you did know what to do?"

Notice the "what if" question is a rephrasing of that person's statement.

We can learn to listen to ourselves better too:

"I don't know where to turn."

"What if I did know where to turn?"

Deep listening opens hearts and minds to see and understand things we couldn't see or understand before.

Master the Art of Deep Listening

The heart of the discerning acquires knowledge,
for the ears of the wise seek it out.

Proverbs 18:15

The effective leader consciously develops the art of listening well, and of holding the space for their team to listen to one another. Note the verse says, "for the ears of the wise seek it out" – it doesn't say "for the tongue to tell them what to do."

Listening deeply means we can respectfully mine the knowledge, experience and imaginations of our team, to collaboratively find what's needed. Creative solutions pop to the surface when people have the space to "think aloud".

Are your wise ears seeking out the knowledge of your team? You discover it by using respectful listening and incisive questions, that can slice to the heart of the matter. To develop the super-power of wise listening you need to park our own story, opinion and agenda, so that you can listen with an open attitude of compassionate curiosity.

Listening isn't about just pressing the pause button on your monologue.

Anon.

Time to reflect:

What in the one thing that most challenges you about listening wisely?

What do you choose to do about that?

How well are you listening to yourself?

What small do-able step can you take today to better listen to your Wisdom?

What difference could that make to your business and to your life?

Listening wisely, and being deeply listened to, can help us tune in to our own experience and to that of our team. But what can help us find a way forward in the business when anxiety threatens to overwhelm and we become trapped in procrastination and overwhelm?

Chapter 45

Break Free from Anxiety, Procrastination and Overwhelm

Recently I read Tim Grahl's book *Running Down a Dream - your road map to winning creative battles.*

Aren't we all chasing a dream and trying to win creative battles, no matter what our line of business? I love this book because he speaks so frankly of his own journey to success; how "fear demons" rose up at different stages of his journey as he became a world-renowned author and book marketing expert. Newsflash! **It is on the brink of success that our deepest, darkest and most terrifying fear demons emerge!**

Anxiety can erode our self-confidence and our motivation. And when anxiety overwhelms us, we're likely to duck for cover - to not do the work we are called to do. We hide under the "slacker" blanket of procrastination. Fear can overwhelm and cripple us:

> *A sluggard says, 'There's a lion in the road,*
> *a fierce lion roaming the streets!'*

Proverbs 26:13

(This is almost a repeat of Proverbs 22:13 - things are reiterated when a point is being emphasised!)

We frighten ourselves; we dissuade ourselves with imagined difficulties - as though there is a lion waiting to devour us. We feel overwhelmed. We hunker down; we don't venture out into the world of work. We make excuses; we act busy when we know we aren't actually doing anything that moves us forward.

> *As a door turns on its hinges,*
> *so a sluggard turns on his bed.*
>
> **Proverbs 26:14**

I love the humour here. A door moves but it's going nowhere!

(Here is succinct storytelling - marketing at its finest; a clear and engaging image and message created in only a few words).

Perhaps it's time to recognise your own unhelpful patterns of behaviour and turn to Wisdom. There are work challenges; but there is no lion - or wolf - at the door. It is an illusion. Even if circumstances are tough right now, trust that when you are walking in the path of Wisdom, there is a way forward! Recognise that the sense of overwhelm is fed by the negative stories you are imagining. Don't remain in a static place. Rather, envisage yourself generating a stable and satisfying income. Connect with your support team, who can help you break through that which has you trapped. Seek Wisdom, and get working on your business. **With action comes clarity.**

Anxiety is a bad master and will impede our progress if we allow it to take control. Recognising and acknowledging the anxiety we experience, without allowing it to crack the whip, can be the first step from procrastination and overwhelm to competence and confidence. Whilst anxiety can overwhelm, it can also be helpful. Its tug in our stomach can alert us to possible danger. It can be a helpful servant that nudges us to take action to avoid a potentially damaging situation. So, our challenge is to listen to anxiety, without allowing it to take control.

The biggest risk is not taking any risk at all.

Mark Zuckerberg

Time to reflect:

What most challenges you in this chapter?

What "lions" are frightening you?

What gives you courage to take action?

What doable step will you take today to move your business forward?

What difference could that make to your business and to your life?

Another equally powerful block to success can be our own anger. So, what does Solomon offer about how to manage anger?

Chapter 46

How to Ensure Anger Does Not Crack the Whip

Anxiety has a more exuberant and vocal twin - anger. Uncontrolled anger can blow relationships apart - at home, and in the business. It wreaks havoc in relationships. But it's helpful to remember the feeling of anger is not the problem in itself.

Our feelings are never wrong as long as we never use them as a weapon against anyone, including ourselves.

Anonymous

When anger erupts onto the stage of my life, if I peek behind the scenes, I spot anxiety, fear or disappointment in the wings. What is really going on for me? What might be going on for the other person? What might be feeding the anger? Each one of us can cast ourselves in the role of the aggressor, the victim or the hero who overcomes life's challenges. The choice is ours.

When we feel anger rising, we need to stop and ask ourselves what is the change we need. Is there an issue we need to address? Are we feeding ourselves thoughts that fuel our irritation or do we need to deal with a boundary issue? It's how we go about creating the change we need that makes the difference. Hurt and discord happen when we allow the feeling of anger to erupt into aggressive behaviour. Our emotions are good servants but bad masters. Listen to what your anger is telling you, but take time to cool off before addressing the issue. Don't be quick to react.

A quick-tempered person does foolish things,

Proverbs 14:17a

Foolish things hurt relationships. And foolish things are often ethically irresponsible. Solomon didn't know about Neuroscience, but he intuitively knew that acting out of anger has bad consequences. What we now know is that when we're angry our brains are hijacked into survival mode and the prefrontal cortex is temporarily offline. This means our ability to see another perspective, to perceive options and to consider possible consequences is seriously impaired. **Acting out of anger is dangerous for relationships and perilous for business.**

When we choose Wisdom, we decide there's more to life than seeking revenge.

Do not say, "I'll do to them as they have done to me;
I'll pay them back for what they did."

Proverbs 24:29

We can use our relational skills to create happier, healthier options. But when we choose to speak or act aggressively, we risk enraging others.

A gentle answer turns away wrath,
but a harsh word stirs up anger.

Proverbs 15:1

Anger stirred up is not easily quenched, and it shuts down meaningful relationship.

A brother wronged is more unyielding than a fortified city;
disputes are like the barred gates of a citadel.

Proverbs 18:19

There are those who love a quarrel. Those who feed on the adrenalin rush of the upset; who enjoy the attention they get from stirring up trouble.

> *Whoever loves a quarrel loves sin;*
> *Whoever builds a high gate invites destruction.*
>
> **Proverbs 17:19**

Quarrels will happen, because we won't always see things the same way. **All conflict is a protest at the disconnection we are experiencing.** But do we *love* a quarrel? Do we instigate quarrels for no good reason, or cling tightly to them and refuse to let them go? This verse could be translated as, "Whoever loves a quarrel loves missing the mark." When we love a quarrel, we disconnect from the other person and from values of care, compassion, forgiveness and respect. We miss the mark of being the best we can be.

In holding on to quarrels we build "high gates" - we make it impossible for the quarrel to be repaired - for the relationship to be restored. If we love a quarrel, ultimately there will be unfortunate consequences.

> *… the rod they wield in fury will be broken.*
>
> **Proverbs 22:8b**

The feeling of anger is not the problem; it's our aggressive actions that stem from feeling frustrated which cause the problem, and, at some point, there will be a consequence for aggressive action.

This proverb can challenge us at a personal level, and can also impact our business. We can choose a rod of fury or a conductor's rod that orchestrates harmony. We'll look at dealing wisely with conflict in the next chapter.

It is often the thoughts we focus on which cause anxiety or anger to take control.

> *… for as he thinks within himself, so he is,*
>
> **Proverbs 23:7 footnote** *a*

Our emotions are impacted by our thoughts.

It's not fair. Why is their business getting all the good press!

When we allow ourselves to dwell on miserable thoughts about another situation, we feed the negative emotion. **When anger or anxiety seize control, we end up in reactivity - and far from Wisdom.** It's not possible to just stop a thought but, as soon as we become aware of an unhelpful thought, we can consciously change that thought. Take a few minutes to test that thought: *"Do I know for sure that what I'm thinking is really true?"* Assess whether or not this thought is winding you up. Change the channel of your thoughts anytime you get hooked on negativity and you will change your emotions and your mood. And that can massively impact your business.

When dealing with people, remember that you are not dealing with creatures of logic, but creatures of emotion.

Dale Carnegie

Time to reflect:

What is your greatest challenge with anger - swallowing it and not saying what you need - or exploding?

What is your greatest awareness in reading this chapter?

What do you choose to do with that awareness?

What difference could that make to your business and to your life?

So, how we deal with anger - whether our own or others' - can greatly impact the outcomes we achieve, but how do we move from conflict to connection?

Chapter 47
From Conflict to Connection

Conflict can happen when there's difference of opinion. And in every organisation, there's bound to be difference of opinion at some point - whether it's with team members, employees, providers or customers. Business is about relationships. And we get to hone our relationships skills in our everyday lives.

Better a dry crust with peace and quiet
than a house full of feasting, with strife.

Proverbs 17:1

Peace is not an absence of conflict, it is the ability to handle conflict by peaceful means.
Ronald Reagan

Peace is an active harmony, where discord has been recreated into melody. Conflict happens in every relationship. We all experience conflict in our lives because conflict is a protest at the disconnection. But because we are so often focused on being "right" we try to persuade the other to see our viewpoint. We focus on the upset itself, or trying to prove the other person wrong.

Relationships work better when we seek to understand where the disconnection has happened. We will recreate harmony far more quickly when we consciously repair the breakdown in communication and connection. **Rupture-and-repair is the pattern of relationship.** Here's how we can restore peace.

Starting a quarrel is like breaching a dam;
so drop the matter before a dispute breaks out.

Proverbs 17:14

A small crack in a dam wall can lead to total devastation. All that had been built up can swiftly be swept away. Once the dam begins to break it is nearly impossible to stop the damage. And often the breach occurs because we insist that we are right – which makes the other person wrong!

Judith Glaser states that we have an addiction with being right.[82] When we are insistent on proving we are right we lose focus on the relationship. **We can choose to be right or we can choose to heal the rupture and be in relationship.** Repair the crack before the dam wall ruptures.

Dealing with Conflict

A person's wisdom yields patience;
it is to one's glory to overlook an offence.

Proverbs 19:11

The wise person recognises that not every issue is worth starting a quarrel.

The way of the Lord is a refuge for the blameless,

Proverbs 10:29a

So, what can a person do to avoid conflict? Focus on your own behaviour. What was your part in the upset? It takes two to tango. Is ego encouraging you to fire all your artillery - to attack with all guns blazing? Or is your shadow ego telling you not to make a fuss - urging you to deny what you need? How to create win-win for everyone's well-being? What is Wisdom whispering to you about the conflict? Reflect on your own behaviour. What was your part in causing the disconnection? What is the way to honour integrity and restore peace?

> *Hatred stirs up conflict,*
> *But love covers over all wrongs.*
>
> **Proverbs 10:12**

Are you focused on hatred - that stirs up dissension - or are you focused on love? To paraphrase Scott Peck, "Love is extending yourself to cause the other person's growth." [83]Are you using conflict as an opportunity for growth - both for the other person and for yourself?

> *Drive out the mocker, and out goes strife;*
> *quarrels and insults are ended.*
>
> **Proverbs 22:10**

We could read that as, "Drive out the one who attacks, or who treats others with ridicule or contempt, and out goes angry and bitter disagreement; quarrels and insults are ended." If there is an ongoing behaviour pattern of conflict within the organisation, identify if there is a common source, deal with the issue and "drive it out".

That does not literally mean to drive the person out – is something needed to change their behaviour? There is a time to recognise that some people aren't members of the work-team and maybe it is time to let them go – and, of course, always abide by legal requirements regarding fair practice to employees.

> *Without wood a fire goes out;*
> *without a gossip a quarrel dies down.*
>
> **Proverbs 26:20**

PeopleSpeak: Don't add fuel to the fire.

Entertaining gossip about a conflict is never okay. Beware the person who adds fuel to the fire and creates havoc in the team. And make sure that person isn't you!

Like one who grabs a stray dog by the ears
is someone who rushes into a quarrel not their own.

Proverbs 26:17

It is dangerous to get involved in other people's conflicts. Imagine trying to grab a stray dog by the ears - you're likely to get bitten!

PeopleSpeak: Keep your nose out of people's business or it may come back to bite you.

Enemies disguise themselves with their lips,
but in their hearts they harbour deceit.
Though their speech is charming, do not believe them,
for seven abominations fill their hearts.
Their malice may be concealed by deception,
but their wickedness will be exposed in the assembly.

Proverbs 26:24-26

Don't be fooled by smooth talk. It is believed that the number "seven" signifies an indeterminate amount, so there are innumerable deceits in the hearts of those who would work against you. The warning here is that enemies may seem to be friends at first. Listen to your intuition and watch for patterns - notice who is the common denominator in conflict and unrest, and you will uncover who is the deceiver in your midst - the trickster who could sabotage your big dream.

For as churning cream produces butter,
and as twisting the nose produces blood,
so stirring up anger produces strife.'

Proverbs 30:33

When butter is made, you can't reverse the process. When blood has been spilt, you can't unspill it. Aggressive action, whether slow and deliberate or quick and impulsive, will have significant outcomes that can't be undone.

How to Heal Conflict

Wisdom is found on the lips of the discerning,
but a rod is for the back of one who has no sense.

Proverbs 10:13

Discernment means we assess what is needed before we do or don't speak. **Pausing to think about what is needed is an essential Wisdom practice.** We can pay a punishing price - a rod for the back - when we are careless with how and when we use our words.

Peoplespeak: Put your brain into gear before you engage your lips.

… violence overwhelms the mouth of the wicked.

Proverbs 10:6b

In some translations this reads as "the mouth of the wicked conceals violence."[84]

Careless words and lack of listening lead to conflict. Solomon is clear that the "mouth of the fool" (someone with poor judgment) causes trouble.

… a chattering fool comes to ruin.

Proverbs 10:8b

… the mouth of a fool invites ruin.

Proverbs 10:14b

So, what do fools do? They talk unnecessarily:

Sin [missing the mark] is not ended by multiplying words,

Proverbs 10:19a

Using more words doesn't build a bridge between people. It doesn't heal the disconnection. **When conflict happens, we need to listen deeply.** We need to regain trust and find out what triggered distrust. We intuitively sense when there is dishonesty or a lack of transparency. We sense judgement or aggression in a person's attitude, even if it's not consciously evident in their behaviour. Glaser explains how trust or distrust are assessed in different regions the brain.[85] Distrust is registered in the amygdala - the part of the brain that triggers a "fight or flight" reaction. This part of the brain makes an instant assessment of distrust. And what we know from neuroscience is that when this part of the brain is triggered the "thinking brain" - the prefrontal cortex - goes temporarily "off-line". In other words, a reaction of distrust is instinctive and immediate. And when we experience distrust, we will be locked into either/or, dualistic thinking; we won't be able to see nuances, to perceive other perspectives or possibilities.

A perverse person stirs up conflict,
and a gossip separates close friends.

Proverbs 16:28

A person whose behaviour is perverse - unaccommodating, inflexible and judgemental - erodes trust. And that means conflict will happen.

For relationships where people thrive, we need to develop the art of listening and talking wisely - of being relationally intelligent, so we can understand each other's perspectives, values and agendas.

The one who has knowledge uses words with restraint,
and whoever has understanding is even-tempered.

Proverbs 17:27

The Power of Forgiveness

When you're leading a team, **mistakes will sometimes happen, because people are human. It's how we respond when someone messes up that makes the difference.**

Whoever would foster love covers over an offence,
but whoever repeats the matter separates close friends.

Proverbs 17:9

The chapter on *Listening Wisely* can be a helpful reminder to find a way to re-establish connection when a relationship is ruptured. Relational skill is essential to turn the crisis of conflict into opportunity for reconnection and greater insight.

You don't have to jump into every briar patch you see.
(I don't know who originally said that, but I could hear that rolling off Brer Rabbit's tongue!)

Time to reflect:

What do you need to become aware of to ensure you do not let unhelpful words slip from your mouth?

What can you do to repair the ruptures in your relationships?

What difference could that make to your business and to your life?

In challenging situations, intuition can guide us to what's needed. But isn't intuition just "fluffy stuff" – or does it have scientific credibility?

Chapter 48

Intuition - Tuning into Inner Knowing

We started this book with a glance at Indiana Jones' astute mindset that, together with his courage, gives him the edge over others seeking the same precious objects. Deciphering the seemingly invisible clues saves Indiana from danger. He outsmarts the villains and discovers the treasure. He doesn't have the latest gadgets but he has an inner knowing that keeps him on track, that protects him from danger and guides him to reach his goal. In this chapter we'll look at the power of intuition within the world of business.

The hearts of the wise make their mouths prudent,

Proverbs 16:23a

Notice, again, this verse says it is the *heart,* and not the mind, that leads to wise words. Neuroscience has discovered that our brains aren't only in our heads. Vital *knowing* is processed in our hearts!

Pay attention and turn your ear to the sayings of the wise;
apply your heart to what I teach,
for it is pleasing when you keep them in your heart …

Proverbs 22:17, 18a

Note, it does not say, "Keep them in your *mind.*" **For strategic decisions, we need a deep heart-sense of what matters.**

The heart has its reasons of which reason knows nothing.
Blaise Pascal More Blaise

Body Awareness

Intuition is sometimes perceived as "fluffy stuff". Interestingly, internationally recognised neuroscientist Dr Daniel Siegel discusses the power of intuition in several of his books and describes it as a hub of awareness.[86] In other words, intuition is a scientifically observable human faculty. He explains how we receive messages from our five senses - seeing, hearing, our senses of touch, taste and smell - and then mentions three other senses. He refers to our sixth sense as our somatic "knowing" – we recognise signals like the tension of our muscles, a knot in our gut, a constriction in our throats.

By listening to our bodies, we become more attuned to our emotions, to what's unfolding, and how we are interpreting these signals. For example, in a difficult conversation, I might notice a tension in my jaws. I ask myself, "What is my body telling me?" Or I might notice a facial expression or sudden shift in the other person's body position. I ask myself, "What might this be telling me?" This helps me to be aware of my inner knowing and to the other person's experience. Somatic knowing is a form of intuition. The most helpful training I have done that has heightened my awareness of my own reactions and that of others has been NLP - Neuro Linguistic Programming.

By having the affirmation that neuroscience makes sense of our heartfelt response and our "gut feel" we can gain confidence in tuning in to this inner knowing. Often, we are aware of someone's intentions because we have observed their body language, even though this may not have been at a conscious level. Science explains our innate ability to read micro-gestures which flit over a person's face so fast we don't consciously register them, yet we know that we know.[87]

In the last couple of decades there have been some insightful books published about understanding Body Language. I particularly recommend Navarro's *What Every Body Is Saying*. This is my favourite "body language" book because he relates his observations to neuroscience, helping us to use body cues to make sense of a person's intentions or emotional state.

Of course, awareness of body language isn't anything new. For example, in Proverbs 6:13 Solomon observes the "wink of the eye", the "signals with the feet" and "motions with his fingers." This reference to the feet aligns with Navarro's observation that a person's feet and legs are one of the most accurate indicators of their intention. For example, are the person's feet turned towards you or away? Are they relaxed or poised for fight or flight?

We register body language at a subconscious level. **We can increase our awareness in any interaction, by asking ourselves, "How do I know what I know?"**

Whoever winks their eye is plotting perversity;
whoever purses their lips is bent on evil.

Proverbs 16:30

Observing Language

Another aspect of intuition is indicated on the seventh sense on Siegel's hub, which he describes as "aspects of the mind". These include paying attention to the words that we and others use, and the thoughts and images that spring into our minds. We can also heighten our intuition by becoming more aware of what is unsaid.

By paying attention to verbal signals we enlarge our awareness. For example, a team member says, "We're up against a brick wall". It's easy to let such a comment slip by - but being aware of the metaphor can help us to discover what is stopping us from moving forward and what is needed to remedy this. I might respond, "It feels like we're up against a brick wall. Tell me more." By acknowledging the expression used by the person and taking time to reflect on those particular words, we often gain deeper insight into what is stopping us, what's needed to overcome the obstacle or what has the potential to unfold.

Sense of Connection

Intuition is also strengthened by our inner attunement - which is the eighth sense on Siegel's hub of awareness. At times, we have a sense of "feeling felt" by others. This increases our sense of connection not only to the other person, but also to our sense of belonging to the larger picture of what it means to be human. When we acknowledge another's thoughts and perceptions, and respond to how they are feeling, it deeply impacts the quality of conversation and builds the foundation of trust that is essential for collaboration. As entrepreneurs, we can use this awareness to build a strong and loyal team, as well as develop a following of loyal customers who will feel understood and supported when we are attuned.

How to listen deeply to your team and gently coach them to listen to each other? Read Nancy Kline's book *Time to Think - listening to ignite the human mind* for a good start. Or work with an *accredited* life coach or take a training course as a life coach. I stress the word "accredited" because there are people who claim to be coaches but who do the talking - who "tell you what to do". This is because they do not have the training and expertise to educe the client's knowledge and discernment.

Working with a skilled coach can help you to think more clearly about what's needed in your business and in your life. And it will also give you the opportunity to observe the art of deep listening, so you can train yourself in these skills, because listening well is an attitude and a skill we can learn. And what this means is you will gain valuable skills that will enhance your ability to create an effective team and happy customers, as well as develop your own clear thinking about your business.

Beyond Human Understanding

…from the LORD comes the proper answer of the tongue.

Proverbs 16:1b

Whether we can fully explain it or not, intuition is a gift.

The lips of a king speak as an oracle,

Proverbs 16:10a

Could we perceive this proverb as:

the [intuitive] leader brings a wise and sometimes mysterious message from God, the source of Wisdom.

What message do we bring that those in the business world need to hear?

People with high levels of personal mastery...cannot afford to choose between reason and intuition, or head and heart, any more than they would choose to walk on one leg or see with one eye.

Peter Senge

Time to reflect:

Think of a time when you had a strong "gut feel" about a situation?

How did you know what you knew?

Take a coffee break in a relaxed environment where you can watch people. Notice people's body language. What messages can you read, without being able to hear the conversation?

Reflect on Siegel's eight senses. What aspects of your intuition do you desire to strengthen?

What small doable step can you take today to increase your awareness and intuition?

What are your thoughts about divine inspiration?

What difference could that make to your business and to your life?

Before we begin to explore how our relationships can impact us, let's take a quick recap of our discoveries about the awesome treasure of IQ, EQ and more.

Chapter 49

Going for Gold

In the opening minutes of "Raiders of the Lost Ark" Marion Ravenwood is holding snowballs to her temples. She has just out-drunk a giant of a man in her bar. Is she trying to cool the heat in her head? An unmistakable shadow appears on the wall. We *know* it's Indiana! The adventure begins. Indiana outwits the Nazi thugs, escapes the snake-infested crypt with Marion and causes havoc on the airstrip, to stop the power of the Ark falling into the hands of evil. Indiana isn't an effusive talker yet we sense he stands for freedom, frankness and honesty. We know he will succeed in his mission despite the odds. Indiana is a character we intuitively trust. His innate qualities inspire us.

Like our movie hero, we need to be careful with our words. Indiana does not let anxiety overwhelm him. How could he be the hero if he did! He uses his sense of anger to take righteous action, but he doesn't let his emotions seize control.

Whilst Indiana relies on quick thinking in the moment of danger, one senses that there is also within him the capacity for "slow thinking" - the power of intuition and deep awareness.

... for the ears of the wise seek it out.

Proverbs 18:15b

Our wise listening can unlock an Indiana type of possibility thinking, no matter how bleak a situation may seem.

Sometimes we don't know what we think, or we haven't processed our thoughts adequately to see a clear line of what we need to do. At times, we might not have considered the possible consequences of an action. Or we haven't broadened or deepened our thinking, or thought laterally about what's on our minds. We need someone to create the safe space and to listen deeply so we can hear ourselves think.

Sometimes, this is at an individual level, but things can get exciting when a team leader has the skills to guide team members to listen deeply to each other. And this quality of conversation only unfolds when there is a strong sense of trust. **Proverbs encourage us to be *heart* people.**

Learning to talk wisely and learning to listen deeply can be the most valuable assets you can ever gain.

Deep listening can release synergistic thinking that breaks through the business stratosphere to previously undreamed possibilities.

Be patient toward all that is unsolved in your heart and try to love the questions themselves, like locked rooms and like books that are now written in a very foreign tongue.

Ranier Maria Rilke[88]

So, both at an individual and business level, **how can we *be* the difference that *makes* the difference?**

Be the Difference
That Makes the Difference

Chapter 50

The Power of Healthy Relationships

Solomon answers one of the greatest questions we can ever ask:

How can we live well?

He gives a map to follow. Success can be found. And part of the code that unlocks true success is our relationships. Building relationship is key to team motivation, even with your virtual assistant. And every wise business person knows that people buy from people they like and trust. Successful marketing isn't only about having a good product or service to sell. This means that reflecting on how to build healthy relationship is essential for both our personal well-being as well as our prosperity.

Qualities of Healthy Relationship

Like a bird that flees its nest
is anyone who flees from home.

Proverbs 27:8

A nest signifies comfort, safety and security.

Solomon speaks of respecting one's parents, of the relationship with one's life partner, and of preparing one's children for life.

Listen to your father, who gave you life,
and do not despise your mother when she is old.

Proverbs 23:22[89]

Derek Draper, author of *Create Space – How to Manage Time, and Find Focus, Productivity and Success* proposes that how we view our relationships makes a huge difference to how fulfilling or irritating those relationships are.[90] **In essence, loyalty is a choice, and a code for life.**

Do not forsake your friend or a friend of your family,

Proverbs 27:10a

These verses remind me of *Running Down a Dream* by Tim Grahl. He shares how his wife stands by him yet challenges him to follow his heart's calling, and to bring his vision into reality. **A true friend is open and honest yet doesn't attempt to control the other.**

Wounds from a friend can be trusted,
but an enemy multiplies kisses.

Proverbs 27:6

It makes sense that constructive criticism can be painful, but recognise its value when it comes from one who has your best intentions at heart.

Perfume and incense bring joy to the heart,
and the pleasantness of a friend
springs from their heartfelt advice.

Proverbs 27:9

As Richard Branson says, we need friends and family whose wit, charm and wisdom help us keep our feet on the ground while we look at the stars. [91]

What Erodes Relationship

In the course of his work as a judge or magistrate Solomon probably observed how marriages fall apart.

> *Better to live on a corner of the roof*
> *than share a house with a quarrelsome wife.*
>
> **Proverbs 25:24**

> *A quarrelsome wife is like the dripping*
> *of a leaky roof in a rainstorm;*
>
> **Proverbs 27:15**

In an unhappy relationship home is no longer a place of comfort and rest.

Solomon describes a situation that is almost impossible to overcome.

> *Anger is cruel and fury overwhelming,*
> *but who can stand before jealousy?*
>
> **Proverbs 27:4**

Anger and jealousy erode a relationship.

> *Better is open rebuke*
> *than hidden love.*
>
> **Proverbs 27:5**[92]

Can jealousy in relationship be "hidden love"? In these verses, jealousy is juxta-positioned to sincerity and openness.

And Solomon advises against flattery:

If anyone loudly blesses their neighbour early in the morning,
it will be taken as a curse.

Proverbs 27:14

He says wealth can attract false friends but poverty can erode even genuine relationships.[93]

Company to Avoid

Within the Proverbs, Solomon talks about whose company to avoid: the glutton,[94] the adulterer, and those who drink heavily.

Avoiding the company of certain people may sound as though you're thinking too much of yourself but that is advice given in many self-development books: if you want to be successful, hang out with successful people.

Peoplespeak: Birds of a feather flock together.

Creating Healthy Relationship in the Workplace

How we treat others will come back to us. **As violence begets violence so kindness begets kindness.** Treat people with consideration and respect - whether they are the cleaner, the employee, the team member, the customer or the funder.

Whoever digs a pit will fall into it;
if someone rolls a stone, it will roll back on them.

Proverbs 26:27

Peoplespeak: What goes around comes around.

I begin to understand Peter Drucker's statement that "culture eats strategy for breakfast." The culture of our work is entirely dependent on the relationships we build. And it is a healthy culture, not strategy, that creates trust, loyalty, and an empowering environment where people find meaning in work and where cutting-edge innovation can thrive. Are we creating work cultures that support better, healthier lives for all the team?

Don't focus on closing a sale, focus on opening a relationship.

Michelle Stonhill

Time to reflect:

What words would you use to describe the quality of your work relationships?

How would you rate the sincerity, openness, trust and loyalty in your significant relationships?

Are there any factors that are eroding your relationships, and, if so, what can you do to improve them?

What difference could that make to your business and to your life?

So, what is the essential element every leader needs to embrace to create a culture of trust?

Chapter 51
Why Boundaries Matter

A s business leaders we have a responsibility to ensure the well-being of others, as related to our business. Well-being is directly related to respect, and respect is upheld by healthy limits. We need to know and guard the values that ensure successful business.

The one who guards a fig tree will eat its fruit,
and whoever protects their master will be honoured.

Proverbs 27:18

Whatever the situation, personal or business, we won't eat the fruit - reap the reward - unless we guard our priorities and our values. Holding boundaries in the workplace is staking what is needed for the business to thrive. It is not about controlling other people. **The wise leader gives clear limits and creates a climate of trust, collaboration and accountability that enables every employee to thrive.**

… preserve sound judgement and discretion;

Proverbs 3:21b

I notice the word "preserve". It's a verb - a *doing* word. This indicates that judgement and discernment develop through deliberate, conscious action - not as an unexpected by-product.

In ancient civilisations, preserving was an essential skill. Without fridges or freezers, every household would have relied on traditional methods of preserving to ensure a food supply through lean periods when fresh food was scarce. Preservation is a careful process that takes time to ensure the quality of the product is maintained. In the same way, maintaining sound judgment doesn't happen by chance - we need to *preserve* it.

We are advised, "Do not let wisdom and judgement out of your sight."[95] We need sound judgment and discernment with us wherever we are, in every situation, to make wise decisions. For each of us, in every aspect of our lives, we need to discern and maintain clear boundaries, regarding the manner we use and share our time, space, possessions and money.

Boundaries in Business

Remember our discussion about the slacker,[96] whose field was overrun with weeds?

Like a city whose walls are broken through
is a person who lacks self-control.

Proverbs 25:28

The stone wall was in ruins. As the successful farmer needs well-maintained fences to preserve his assets, and the city is not safe without strong walls, we need limits within the workspace too.

For the successful business-person this is knowing what belongs in work and what doesn't.

Who does the task belong to?

And who does it not belong to?

What is needed, where and by when?

There is a time to clearly indicate when someone oversteps the limit. We can do this without demeaning, degrading or labelling, providing we ensure that anger has not taken control. Our anger rises when our limits are not respected. Anger is a signal we need change; that too much of ourselves has been compromised.[97] You may find it helpful to re-read chapter 46: "How to Ensure Anger Does Not Crack the Whip".

Effective boundaries are needed.

Like apples of gold in settings of silver
is a ruling rightly given.
Like an earring of gold or an ornament of fine gold
is the rebuke of a wise judge to a listening ear.

Proverbs 25:11,12

This proverb gives images which convey beauty and wealth. A wise rebuke adds to the value; it does not destroy. The person with the "listening ear" heeds advice on clear and fair boundaries and gains the benefit. And, as we've discussed regarding conversational skills, the wise leader handles situations in a way that promotes trust, that creates the opportunity for dialogue, so everyone's voices are heard.

If we don't act on our own behalf, we will lose spirit, resourcefulness, energy, health, perspective and resilience.

Anne Katherine

Time to reflect:

What boundaries need reassessment in your business?

What boundaries need reassessment to maintain healthy balance between your work and personal life?

What small doable step will you take today / this week to assess/strengthen your boundaries?

What difference could that make to your business and to your life?

It isn't easy to be a wise leader, even within a team of one, so how does one figure out what to do, how to do – and when?

Chapter 52

The Amazing Power of Discretion

My friend Frank is a cancer survivor. One side of his face drags downward - the result of necessary drastic surgery. He doesn't have a beautiful face but he has a keen sense of humour; he is clever, astute and a sincere, warm-hearted friend. Once you know Frank you don't notice the disfigurement - his brilliant personality beams through. Just as Forest Gump said, "Stupid is as stupid does", beauty is as beauty does. My friend Frank is beautiful in his own unique way.

As Solomon was a mega-wealthy leader, he was no doubt introduced to many beautiful women. It is interesting what he has to say on this subject:

> *Like a gold ring in a pig's snout*
> *is a beautiful woman who shows no discretion.*
>
> **Proverbs 11:22**

This is the opposite of my friend Frank - apparent outward beauty but nothing shines from within. Beauty without discretion is as incongruous as a gold ring in a pig's snout.

What is discretion? Knowing how to skilfully and meaningfully interact with others, always upholding trust. Compare this observation with Proverbs 11:16 which says a kind-hearted woman gains honour [respect]. And remember, this was written in an era and culture where women were not treated equally. It is our inner qualities that earn people's appreciation. Wisdom is the essence of inner beauty and relies on discernment.

Discretion will protect you,

Proverbs 2:11a

Discernment is the ability to distinguish good from bad - being careful about what you do and how you do it, so you do not cause harm.[98] In supporting others, we support ourselves. Consider this: not only in the sense of us as individuals within our businesses, but what about its significance at a community, national and global level? Discretion guides us to decide what should be done in a particular situation. It guides us to set helpful boundaries for our own and others' well-being. It gives us choice, judgement and freedom.

When we are successful in business, life doesn't get simpler or easier; there are many far-reaching decisions to be made. The more successful we are, the more we need discretion and discernment. With greater power comes greater responsibility. And with greater power and responsibility, we need greater response-ability. We need the ability to respond in a way that builds bridges between people and makes a difference in society. As successful business-people, we have the capacity to be transformers for good.

The ability to make wise, responsible decisions will protect us. Understanding will guard us.

Discernment Leads to Understanding

It is the wise choices we make, with clear understanding that every decision we take has consequences and impacts others, that will keep us from the wrong turns that take us off track. And choosing not to do anything is also a choice. Discretion is the offspring of Wisdom, saving us from the temptations that would take us off-track. Think of "the adulteress", Proverbs 2:16 -24, as a metaphor.

What tempts us? What infatuates us? What could seduce us? Lust? Greed? Power? Unhealthy relationships? What discernment do we need to avoid these snares?

Too often we, as society, have looked down on those less privileged or less able than ourselves, including the poor, the less literate, and, sometimes, even our own children. What would happen if we treated all people as deserving of equal respect? Jesus Christ was the ultimate transformer, because, to him, each person was a unique individual who mattered, no matter their background, their challenges, or the choices they had made.

Discernment is about the considering the alternatives. The choices we make ultimately lead us on one path or another. Our decisions lead to our downfall - or to fulfilment and success. The choice is ours.

> *To understand is to stand under*
> *– which is to look up to*
> *– which is a great way to understand.*
>
> Corrita Kent[99]

Time to reflect:

How would those closest to you describe your discretion? What might need your attention?

What would help you gain more discernment in creating the life and business you desire?

What choices do you need to make today?

What is Wisdom whispering to you about these decisions?

What difference could that make to your business and to your life?

Where discernment thrives, Wisdom thrives. Where Wisdom thrives, social justice thrives. Let's discover how.

Chapter 53

Staking Out the Territory of Social Justice

Have you heard of the company Elvis & Kresse? They produce a high-end range of fabulous belts, handbags and other gear - using repurposed fire hose and other products normally dumped in landfill! And they are redefining what "luxury" means because they are committed to a zero-waste ethic and 50% of their profits are donated to charity. Through their example, high-end fashion companies are discovering that the offcuts they are throwing in landfill can instead be creatively used. Kresse says dumping your waste in landfill is like the toddler pushing their toys and junk under the bed and saying they have tided the room.

Elvis & Kresse are modelling ethical, responsible production; at the same time, they are educating companies that throwing stuff in landfill is throwing away profit. They are convincing businesses of the financial and long-term benefits of upcycling - creating functional and beautiful products from that which others toss.

Making a Difference

Remove the dross from the silver,
and a silversmith can produce a vessel;

Proverbs 25:4

Whoever sows injustice reaps calamity,

Proverbs 22:8a

Consider these verses in context to ourselves as a business community. **What calamity are we inviting upon our societies when we support unethical business and political practices?** High tariffs are imposed on desperately poor countries. Exorbitant taxes or interest rates are charged on outstanding debt. Manufacturers do not uphold fair codes of practice for their employees. When we create products or use resources that add to the pollution problem or to the climate issues, we are inviting calamity.

> *… the prudent give thought to their steps.*
>
> Proverbs 14:15b

Prudent is "acting with or showing care and thought for the future."[100] Often, we overlook that our seemingly small decisions may have cumulative, long-term consequences. Recently, I wanted to order new business cards. I spoke to a salesperson who tried to persuade me to order their high-end product. I asked him which was the better product ecologically - and of course it was the plain paper version. But what surprised me was his response,

"Nobody has ever asked me that before!"

Are we thinking not only of our own future but also in light of what is good for our children's children's children? We will make different business decisions if we consider the long-term impact. When we do the right thing, individually and as community, there is a positive knock-on effect.

> *When the righteous prosper, the city rejoices;*
>
> Proverbs 11:10a

> *Through the blessing of the upright a city is exalted,*
>
> Proverbs 11:11a

> *Whoever seeks good finds favour,*
>
> Proverbs 11:27a

When we seek good the return is goodwill.

> *… the righteousness will thrive like a green leaf.*
>
> **Proverbs 11:28b**

This image of a green leaf struck me. One green leaf that thrives soon leads to many green leaves. Leaves do not grow in isolation. **When the righteous thrive, the ethos of mutual respect and care naturally multiplies. Let's grow a forest of goodwill!**

> *Whoever increases wealth by taking interest or profit from the poor amasses it for another, who will be kind to the poor.*
>
> **Proverbs 28:8**

There will be natural consequences! It's a spiritual law.

Making a Difference

> *… whoever builds a high gate invites destruction.*
>
> **Proverbs 17:19b**

Barriers create an "us and them" mindset, rather than a "we" mentality. At the time of writing this, the building of high walls to keep out people in desperate need of help is an issue of hot political debate. A few years ago, in an online forum debating the refugee crisis, a post impacted me with a message I've never forgotten. The post had a photo of the deck of a ship packed with people. The pier beneath was equally packed with people gazing up at the ship. You could sense they were crying out to escape their plight; some were climbing the mooring ropes in their desperation to get on board the departing vessel. And the post said something along the lines of:

"Refugees trying to invade us? No! This is a photo of our grandparents, stranded in a foreign country, trying to flee from the invading forces during the Second World War."

The thing is, refugees are people just like us - wanting security; wanting a place to call home; needing not only food and shelter, but dignity and opportunity. We all need compassion, and we need to offer compassion. When we build high walls, we forget we are all humans sharing this planet together. We invite destruction. As Mick Dundee describes in the film *Crocodile Dundee* - it's like two fleas fighting over who owns this patch of the dog.

The generous will themselves be blessed,
for they share their food with the poor.

Proverbs 22:9

Can we, as business leaders, do more to motivate our communities or nations to be generous? Can we give the clarion call for social justice? Are we not called to serve those most in need? **Are we not here to serve our future generations by minding and restoring this beautiful planet?** I know, for me, it's the enormity of the challenges that overwhelms me and sometimes leaves me doing nothing.

… the one who sows righteousness reaps sure reward.

Proverbs 11:18b

Seeds are little, seemingly inconsequential things, that hold a dormant power! What small seeds of righteousness can we begin to germinate in our daily lives? Of course, the big things matter, but there are small, daily acts of kindness we can all make. Little gestures grow to be something much larger that bring their own return.

A ruler who oppresses the poor
is like driving rain that leaves no crops.

Proverbs 28:3

I grew up in Zimbabwe - in my youth it was a land described as the breadbasket of Africa. I have seen the desolation and the famine that is caused when a despot rules. The people's lives are ravaged as well as the land. How do we stand for fair and equal treatment for all?

> *… when the wicked rise to power, people go into hiding.*
>
> **Proverbs 28:12b**

A refugee crisis - people going into hiding - is often the result of bad governance. This line of thought is developed in Proverbs 28.

> *… whoever hardens their heart falls into trouble.*
> *Like a roaring lion or a charging bear*
> *is a wicked ruler over a helpless people.*
> *A tyrannical ruler practices extortion,*
> *but one who hates ill-gotten gain will enjoy a long reign.*
>
> **Proverbs 28:14b-16**

Helping Others Helps Us

> *A gift opens the way*
> *and ushers the giver into the presence of the great.*
>
> **Proverbs 18:16**

When we bring the gift of ourselves and our resources to those in need, to those in danger of harm, and to the voiceless, we open ourselves to divine Love, which flows through us to bless others.

> *Those who give to the poor will lack nothing,*
> *but those who close their eyes to them receive many curses.*
>
> **Proverbs 28:27**

Giving to others by merely opening our wallets does not bring the enrichment that comes from becoming actively involved in helping others. It is in serving others that we learn from them. Others who have endured suffering can help us to see the poverty of mind and soul that has eroded our society.

They can give us gifts of inspiration, generosity, humility, resilience, spirituality and so much more. Mahatma Ghandi was once asked what he thought of Western civilisation, to which he allegedly replied, "I think it would be a good idea."[101]

If you have come here to help me, you are wasting your time.
But if you have come because your liberation is bound up with mine,
then let us work together.

(attributed to Aboriginal activist Lilla Watson)

Time to reflect:

Where do you need to reconsider your business practices and ethics to ensure you are standing for fair and equitable standards?

What contribution are you called to make for social justice - at a local, national or international level?

What steps are you taking today to bring social justice in the situation that is on your heart?

The last chapter of Proverbs returns to the topic of social justice, imploring to speak out for those who cannot speak and to defend the rights of the oppressed and the needy.[102] So what we can learn from Proverbs about social justice?

Chapter 54

Stand for Social Justice

A few years ago, I had the privilege of visiting a very poor rural community in North Eastern Myanmar. The Christian Aid staff worker introduced us to their work, supporting the small local communities to build grain silos. She explained that the peasant people still rely on a barter system; having a supply of rice is like having an ATM they can draw from whenever they need to. This means they have food for themselves, and enough to barter with others, as well as the rice grains that are elemental to sow for the following year's crop. Grain is essential for future yields, so being willing to sell grain enables others to establish economic independence, as well as provide for their immediate needs.

[People] pray God's blessing on the one who is willing to sell [grain].
Proverbs 11:26b

The wise business-person takes a stand for right living and encourages others to do likewise. **Do we apply fair, honest, moral and ethical standards that protect the rights of others and the well-being of society and the planet?** And do we call for upholding these standards in every level of community?

Lao Tzu has been accredited as saying, "If you give a hungry man a fish, you feed him for a day, but if you teach him to fish, you feed him for a lifetime." This adage is true, providing the huge commercial fisheries aren't ravaging the fishing stock!

Here is my interpretation of some of the verses that give instruction regarding treating all people with respect.

Social Justice "do's" from Proverbs

~ The LORD is the Maker of them all. **Proverbs 22:2**

~ Do what is right and just and fair. **Proverbs 1:3b**

~ Save lives. **Proverbs 11:30, 24:11**

~ Seek to understand people's motives, even if we don't agree with their behaviour. **Proverbs 28:21b**

~ Be generous. Share with the poor. **Proverbs 11:25; 22:9**

~ Be honest. Speak the truth. **Proverbs 22:21**

~ Be discerning about the choices you make. **Proverbs 23:2**

~ Convict the guilty. **Proverbs 24:24**

~ Be kind to the poor. **Proverbs 19:17**

And here are social justice "don'ts" from Proverbs:

~ Don't accept bribes to pervert the course of justice. **Proverbs 17:23**

~ Don't show partiality. **Proverbs 24:23; Proverbs 28:21a**

~ Don't oppress the poor to increase your own wealth. **Proverbs 22:16a**

~ Don't take advantage of the poor because they are poor. **Proverbs 22:22a**

~ Don't use legal loopholes to crush the needy. **Proverbs 22:22b**

~ Don't impose fines on the innocent. **Proverbs 17:26a** (Whether it be loan sharks, regarding personal finances or at international levels.)

~ Don't plot against those who live trustfully near you. **Proverbs 3:29** (And aren't we so inter-connected that we all live near each other!)

~ Don't acquit the guilty or condemn the innocent. **Proverbs 17:15** (If we give our business to those who abuse the right of others, or whose policies and practice are ignoring justice or sustainability, are we acquitting the guilty?)

~ Don't change rulings to take advantage of those who cannot represent themselves. **Proverbs 22:28**

Don't take from others what is rightfully theirs. Have we "encroached on the fields" of those who could not defend themselves - robbing people of their rightful legacy? Often, those who are robbed do not have the resources to fight for what is lawfully theirs. How can we use our power as business-people to readdress these social wrongs? We need to take a stand for all people to be treated fairly.

Our First-World Challenge to Address Over-Consumption

When you sit to dine with a ruler,
note well what is before you,
and put a knife to your throat
if you are given to gluttony.
Do not crave his delicacies,
for that food is deceptive.

Proverbs 23:1-3

Don't get caught in desiring what the ultra-wealthy have. Reflect on this in light not only of gluttony of food - but consider mindless consumerism. Are we buying things we really don't need?

These verses caution that what looks like wealth can be deceptive. These "delicacies" don't bring joy. And what is the ultimate cost to our future well-being on this planet? What legacy do we leave for future generations?

… the complacency of fools will destroy them;

Proverbs 1:32b

When we are complacent, we are likely not to take action. **Let's not merely talk about the injustice – let's use our moral compass to DO something that will help to rectify the imbalance!**

Do not exploit the poor because they are poor
and do not crush the needy in court,
for the Lord will take up their case
and will exact life for life.

Proverbs 22:22-23

Peoplespeak: What goes around comes around.

In truth, the world is a seamless web, from which no nation, large or small, young or old, can disassociate itself. Every attitude and every action of every nation can affect the welfare and security of every other nation around the globe.

Robert Kennedy[103]

Time to reflect:

Which one of these "do's" or "don'ts" most challenges you?

What small doable step do you choose to take today?

What difference could that make to your business and to your life?

What difference could that make to the lives of others?

As business people, how can we champion those who cannot speak for themselves?

Chapter 55

Champion Those Who Can't Speak for Themselves

W e can all think of people who have had the courage to stand against wrong-doing that shames or exploits others who do not have the resources to stand for themselves. **Imagine how we, as business leaders, might one day look back and see how we have been champions of the downtrodden.**

Whoever mocks the poor shows contempt for their Maker;

Proverbs 17:5a

People may not be financially poor, but can feel poor in spirit, especially if they have had to endure unkind and unfair public mockery or discrimination. Every leader leads by their example.

[A king's] mouth does not betray justice.

Proverbs 16:10b

Wisdom always stands for honesty, integrity and fairness. Talking about the issues isn't enough.

It's about *doing* the right thing.

The wise prevail through great power,
and those who have knowledge muster their strength;
Surely you need guidance to wage war,
and victory is won through many advisers.

Proverbs 24:5,6

As business leaders, it's time for us to wage war. Not war against people - but war against the issues that are undermining the health of humanity and the stability of the precious and fragile ecosystems on our planet. Together, we need to fight against injustice, poverty, pollution, greed, exploitation and dishonesty. We need to learn from one another, and inspire one another. It's time for collaboration with others and for others.

I remember learning about the French queen Marie Antoinette when I was in school. When she was told the starving peasants had no bread, she was reputed to have said, "Let them eat cake." The French aristocracy's complacency concerning the poverty of the people led to one of the bloodiest revolutions in history.

If you say, 'But we knew nothing about this,'
does not he who weighs the heart perceive it?

Proverbs 24:12a

There are two angles to this. One is that it is our responsibility to be informed.

And secondly, we sometimes are aware of situations that we need to bring to public awareness.

In May 2019 there was a public outcry about the *Jeremy Kyle Show* - a reality TV programme that exposes the sordid details of people's lives. The show has been shut down after a participant took his own life shortly after appearing on the show. Of course, suicide is a complex situation and not due to only one incident. But why don't we make a stand against any behaviour that demeans others?

That is not a series I have followed, but a few years ago I did see an episode. It so incensed me I wanted to write to complain because of the way the presenter derided one of the participants: "You're a disgrace." "You're a loser." I wanted to write and say how harmful attacking the person's character was. The presenter was modelling that it's okay to label, demean, judge and ostracise people. It would have been kinder and more helpful to comment on the person's behaviour: "That behaviour was not okay." A behaviour is something a person can change. But when a person's character is attacked and torn to shreds it is almost impossible for them to believe differently about themselves.

I didn't get to send the letter. I'm sure I wasn't the only one who was concerned about the show. Together, we might have made a difference before tragedy struck.

We need to stand for peace, whatever pressures come against us. Stand for what is right and fair. Yes, there will be the corrupt, the wicked, who will do everything they can to subvert justice. That's when taking action counts the most.

> *Like a muddied spring or a polluted well*
> *are the righteous who give way to the wicked.*
>
> **Proverbs 25:26**

In dry lands when there is little rain, the wild animals become desperately thirsty. As they seek the sparse supply of water, their feet trample the soil into the pool; the watering holes become muddied, but the animals have no other source of water.

For the needy in society, we might be the only "spring" that brings life and hope. Society suffers when charitable organisations are morally polluted. In the next chapter we'll look at our responsibility - and privilege - as leaders in business to do something.

The most powerful memory that stayed with me from my visit to John F Kennedy's grave in the Arlington National Cemetery, a few years ago, was the inscribed quotation on the surrounding wall.

This was part of his inaugural address:

Now the trumpet summons us again.
not as a call to bear arms.
though arms we need.
not as a call to battle though embattled we are.
A call to bear the burden of a long twilight struggle
A struggle against the common enemies of man
- tyranny - poverty - disease - and war itself.

John F Kennedy[104]

(Is that a play on "arms"? Is he referring to the arms on our bodies? We need to *do* something!)

Time to reflect:

As a leader in society, in your community and in your home, what values do you most desire to uphold?

What's the one do-able step can you take today to encourage or empower others - to bring change where it's needed?

What difference could that make to your life and to others' lives?

So, what might this call to "take up arms" mean to us as business owners?

Chapter 56
Light the Torch of Leadership

When we are successful in business we have, possibly without realising it, become leaders. We become leaders in our team, even with our virtual assistants. We become thought leaders through what we share in our writing and social media posts, and through our conversations. What sort of leaders do we choose to be?

As I read Proverbs chapter 16, I noticed a shift in the language. The earlier Proverbs have commented on those who don't have Wisdom - the fool, the adulterer, the sluggard, the wicked. As we move beyond the halfway mark in the book of Proverbs a different focus emerges. Now the word "king" appears. In those days, the king was the ultimate leader. "King" is a position we identify as a powerful leader. Wouldn't these verses come alive for us if we apply them to our leadership!

Qualities of the Wise Leader

Kings detest wrongdoing,
or a throne is established through righteousness.

Proverbs 16:12

We can perceive a throne as a seat of power, that can influence many.

Kings take pleasure in honest lips;
they value the one who speaks what is right.

Proverbs 16:13

Powerful leaders take cognisance of honest words, spoken to uphold right living.

Eloquent lips are unsuited to a godless fool –
how much worse lying lips to a ruler!

Proverbs 17:7

The world seems plagued with political leaders we cannot trust. **The time has come for each one of us, within our own fields, to set the example of leading with integrity.**

… a ruler with discernment and knowledge maintains order.

Proverbs 28:2b

For more on being the leader you want to be, see Chapter 62: "Wisdom - Treasures Beyond Belief".

The Impact of the Leader

Sometimes as leader, even when we seek to establish an environment of equal respect, we do not realise that our mood and behaviour can greatly impact our team far more than that of peers on equal footing. Derek Draper states that a leader's action or inaction has far greater impact on others and on the system than that of other people who are not carrying the same responsibility.[105] Whether we like it or not, there are subconscious power issues - both positive and negative - regarding leadership, both for you and your team. Perhaps that's what Solomon is saying here:

A king's wrath is a messenger of death,
but the wise will appease it.
When a king's face brightens, it means life;
his favour is like a rain cloud in spring.

Proverbs 16:14,15

If you're living in the southern hemisphere a "rain cloud in spring" may sound like a real dampener - pardon the pun. But living in the hot, arid conditions of the biblical setting, this would be a simile for welcome and much-needed refreshment. The team members are impacted by the leader's mood and actions. Whilst obviously not recorded in Proverbs, even the tone of your email can change the quality of the day of the recipients.

In particular, a leader needs to manage their own anger.

> *A king's rage is like the roar of a lion,*
> *but his favour is like dew on the grass.*
>
> **Proverbs 19:12**[106]

Having grown up in Africa, I have memories of nights in the wilds, in a sleeping bag on the ground. I was aware there were no walls of protection as I lay acutely listening to distant roars. Was that a large baboon - no serious concern! Or was that a *lion?* How distant was it? Was it getting closer? My every nerve was taut as I waited for the next roar - trying to assess whether we were safe.

Years later, I worked in a training centre in Africa which was close to the Pretoria Zoo. Often in the late afternoon, the old lion would start to roar. Even though I knew he was behind bars, that sound sent chills down my spine. Be it a memory of a wild animal, or a dominating adult, when we are reminded of a fear-invoking experience, the reptilian part of our brain triggers a fight, flight or freeze reaction. A leader's brusk manner is likely to elicit unhelpful reactive behaviours from team members.

To you, as team leader, you may have thought, "I just spoke a little tersely." To your employee you may have been roaring! **A situation is experienced differently by different people, especially when there is a power differential.**

Conversely, your favour, your acknowledgement, encouragement and affirmation, can feel like dew on the grass. The moisture on the grass in a hot dry climate may be the only hydration for birds and small wild creatures. As leader, your positive and affirming response is refreshing and peaceful to your team; it inspires hope and creates opportunities for new beginnings.

For key aspects on being the leader your team need you to be, check out Section G: "The Awesome Treasure of EQ, IQ and More".

A friend loves at all times,
and a brother is born for a time of adversity.

Proverbs 17:17

In what ways can you be "friend and brother" to those in your team, and encourage them to take responsibility for their own actions? It's easy to blame someone else when things don't go smoothly.

A person's own folly leads to their ruin,
yet their heart rages against the Lord.

Proverbs 19:3

Each time a person stands up for an ideal, or acts to improve the lot of others, or strikes out against injustice, he sends forth a tiny ripple of hope, and crossing each other from a million different centers of energy and daring, those ripples build a current that can sweep down the mightiest walls of oppression and injustice.

Robert Kennedy [107]

Time to reflect:

As a leader, is your presence more like the dew on the grass or the roar of the lion?

What small doable step can you take today to be the leader who inspires the best in your team?

What difference could that make to your business?

What difference could that make to the lives of others?

So how can we, as business leaders, be the ones who wield positive transformative power?

Chapter 57

Wield Transformative Power

I love to read of people whose lives have been remarkable. I admire people who have dared to step outside the box - who have dared to dream of something bigger and better.

Florence Nightingale[108] turned her back on the privileges and confines of being a Victorian lady, and as a young woman became a nurse, despite the disapproval of her parents. She later was a manager and trainer of nurses in the Crimean War and revolutionised the health system. She is venerated as the founder of modern nursing and is responsible for saving thousands, if not millions, of lives.

Martin Luther King sounded a rally cry to stand for justice and equality, and had the courage to live by his convictions.

Nelson Mandela chose to walk the path of forgiveness, connection and communication, in circumstances where many would have chosen hate and violence.

Steve Jobs - I wouldn't be writing this on my MacBook, if a wild teenager hadn't dared to follow his passion.

Oprah Winfrey - despite the disadvantages she faced as a child, she has modelled courage and compassion to millions of people around the world.

Elon Musk - who dared to dream such ridiculous large, audacious dreams he has significantly influenced green technology and he has taken us into a new, previously unimagined dimension of the space age.

They, and many other courageous people, have achieved success - in their different and unique ways. Many have made their lives count - scientists, social justice activists, artists, writers, business people, stay-at-home parents, computer specialists, janitors, nurses, teachers.

Whoever and wherever we are - we can make a difference.

He holds success in store for the upright,

Proverbs 2:7a

Rethinking Righteousness

Righteous sounds boring and judgemental. Righteous could be taken to mean "be compliant: obey the rules of society."

But what if righteous means something radically different? What if *righteous* is about being a rule-breaker - a transformer!

Jesus Christ, one of the most awesome rule-breakers ever, went against the grain of social conformity. He challenged the systems that exploited the poor and needy. He was a magnetic personality. People wanted to be around Jesus! He was always being invited to parties – I imagine that he must have been an inspiring guest! He ignored the dictates of the powerful; he lived by his own inner compass, attuned to Wisdom. He lived in congruence with his values. He lived such a radical life we have measured the calendar by "Before Christ" and "After the Lord". Examine his life and you don't see the wishy-washy person of the Sunday School prayer - "gentle Jesus meek and mild". Rather, you discover a compassionate and powerful person in touch with his calling and his values, who courageously stood for truth, even when it meant making the ultimate sacrifice of dying on the cross.

Merriam Webster describes "righteous" as "setting in accord with divine law - free from guilt or sin". [109]

Reflect on this definition. Imagine living our lives free from a sense of guilt. Imagine living without those nagging "I should have …" "I didn't …" because we are making the *right* choices, that are in alignment with eternal values? Okay, if "sin" means "missing the mark", could we rephrase that as "disconnection"?

If we lived "free from sin / free from missing the mark" wouldn't we be "living free from disconnection"?

(The arrow that misses its mark on the target is disconnected from the bullseye).

Imagine living in connection with the divine, everlasting and ever-present energy of a personal, loving God. Imagine living in connection with yourself, your emotions and your values. Imagine living in connection with those nearest and dearest to you.

Imagine the potential impact if all of us lived without disconnection from the needs of other people. Imagine living without disconnection from all the amazing life forms on this beautiful planet.

Imagine living without disconnection - so that our actions have a positive impact both now and in the future.

What would it be like to live without disconnection? Of course, we will miss the mark time and time again, but when we refocus on living our lives with God in the centre, we'll draw closer to becoming all that we were created to be. It's time to reconnect with the big picture of life and open our eyes to the needs of others. We can be transformers! Imagine the sense of fulfilment if we dare to live fully. Let's live our best lives.

And transformation doesn't happen without creativity. Proverbs 8:22-31 describes the active creativity of the LORD - the "master craftsman". Nothing new is brought into the world without creativity. To be transformers we need to be connected and we need to create!

Take time to reflect on how connected you feel to those things that matter most:

~ In connection with your emotions

~ In connection with your values

~ In connection with your purpose

~ In connection with those nearest and dearest to you

~ In connection with the needs of other people, including those in the remotest parts of the Planet

~ In connection with Joy

~ In connection with Beauty

~ In connection with Creativity and Imagination

~ In connection with Love

~ In connection with the divine, everlasting and ever-present energy of a personal loving God.

How do we connect to God? His divine presence is omniscient - right here with us. Seek Him and you will find Him.

Wisdom holds victory in store for those who live without disconnection. Being in connection is what transforms us, enabling us to become transformers.

> *If your enemy is hungry, give him food to eat;*
> *if he is thirsty, give him water to drink.*
>
> Proverbs 25:21

Be a transformer even when it isn't easy. Be a transformer especially when it isn't easy! With God, all things are possible.

> *The moment one definitely commits oneself, then providence moves too.*
>
> W.H. Murray

Time to reflect:

What do you notice as you reflect on your sense of connection?

What one do-able step can you take today to be in connection with what matters most?

How do you nurture your creativity?

In what ways are you, or could you be, a transformer?

What difference could that make to your business and to your life?

Let's turn back to our friend Indiana Jones, who wields transformative power as easily as he handles his leather whip.

Chapter 58

Going for Gold

Many of the settings of the Indiana Jones movies are in geographic regions where people still live simply, without the sophistication of our Western world. In *Raiders of the Lost Ark* and *The Last Crusade* Indiana single-handedly takes on formidable and powerful groups of Nazis, who are set to rob the indigenous people of their heritage. Whilst audiences enjoy his swashbuckling adventures, there is an element of truth in the seemingly fantastical situations of these movies. Apparently, the Nazis did have a keen interest in archaeology and organised missions to a number of remote locations in their attempt to "prove" their claims of supposed Aryan superiority.[110]

Indiana disrupts their ill-intentioned plans. He stands for doing the right thing - whether it's looking after his dad, challenging the bully or taking on powerful political forces. He is a loyal son and friend, and a citizen who stands for the right thing, despite the danger. He's an inspirational hero. One person with courage, resilience and clear intention that he can make a difference.

Does not he who guards your life know it?
Will he not repay everyone according to what they have done?
Proverbs 24:12

Let's take a quick recap and reflect on our journey in this section. We started with reflecting that healthy relationships are key to living well. We considered the quality of our personal relationships, as well as our virtual and face-to-face connections with our team, colleagues and clients.

We also looked at the need to be aware of social injustice and our responsibility for the health of the planet for future generations. **People care about people who care about people.** Being a person who connects and who is an advocate for doing the right thing matters in building a loyal team and clientele; and it matters if you desire to build a successful business. Anything that has a perennial quality, whether it is a book, a drama, a piece of music or other form of art, or even an organisation lasts because it reaches out to express something that we know has innate truth. If you want to make a life and a business that counts, be prepared to take what you have on hand to wield its potential transformative power for a happier, healthier and safer world. So, if Wisdom is the source of this power, what does that mean for our lives and business?

The Epic Adventure of Business Success

Chapter 59

Seek Wisdom - the Source of All

Many of us start business believing financial wealth is our goal. But Solomon knows there is a far more valuable treasure. He shares one of the greatest secrets of all time: seek Wisdom, not Wealth.

Solomon, one of the wealthiest people who ever lived, guides us to the greatest treasure of all. He's not against Wealth - he had plenty of it! But he understood that Wisdom is of far greater consequence than wealth.

Society's Focus on Wealth

Don't focus on Wealth because:

~ **When we focus on wealth, we're putting our focus in the wrong place.**

> *The wealth of the rich is their fortified city;*
> *they imagine it a wall too high to scale.*

Proverbs 18:11

People might think their wealth will keep them safe; they *imagine* their wealth gives them impenetrable protection.

But circumstances can change overnight. Material security is an illusion.

~ Wealth is transient. In itself, it is of no value when we most need the resources to weather the tough times.

> *Wealth is worthless in the day of wrath,*
>
> **Proverbs 11:4a**

~ Wisdom can transform our entire life circumstances!

> *A prudent servant will rule over a disgraceful son*
> *and will share the inheritance as one of the family.*
>
> **Proverbs 17:2**

~ When we live by Wisdom, we keep balance in our lives. And wealth is a natural outcome.

> *The blessing of the LORD brings wealth,*
> *without painful toil for it.*
>
> **Proverbs 10:22**

What Happened When Solomon Discovered Wisdom?

Solomon's community benefitted from his discernment:

> *The people of Judah and Israel were as numerous as the sand on the seashore;*
> *they ate, they drank and they were happy.*
>
> **1 Kings 4:20**

Solomon lived a well-balanced life.

God gave Solomon wisdom and very great insight,
and a breadth of understanding as measureless as the sand on the seashore.

1 Kings 4:29

Proverbs 10 sums up Wisdom in a few key qualities. Like Solomon, let's choose to integrate these into our lives:

~ be righteous

~ be diligent

~ live with integrity

~ love

~ seek understanding

~ speak and act with discernment.

By wisdom a house is built,
and through understanding it is established;
through knowledge its rooms are filled
with rare and beautiful treasures.

Proverbs 24:3,4

Solomon has cracked the code to living a life that counts. He calls out to us across the chasm of the centuries: "Get Wisdom."[111] He points the way to this abundance. [112] On the walls of history he has inscribed these tenets of Wisdom that are "life to the one who finds them and health to one's whole body."[113]

Building a business is somewhat like creating the universe: it involves both an inner and an outer will. You cannot go wrong if you follow God's example, for God is the ultimate entrepreneur and His enterprise is the universe.

Levi Brackman

Time to reflect:

In choosing the path of Wisdom what has most challenged you?

What is your next step?

What difference could that make to your business and to your life?

So, as we draw near the end, what is the fallout of ignoring Wisdom?

Chapter 60

The Pitfalls of Ignoring Wisdom

When Indiana Jones is on the trail of something mega-important, he often comes across the gruesome remains of those who rushed ahead in their attempt to grab the gold; they paid a huge price because they didn't heed the whispered clues. Here are some of the worst-case scenario outcomes for those who ignore Wisdom.

~ What they dread will overtake them. **Proverbs 10:24**

~ Their hopes come to nothing. **Proverbs 10:28**

~ They will not "remain in the land" - which means that they will have no way of creating sustenance and will not leave a legacy. **Proverbs 10:30**

~ Their words will destroy their whole community. **Proverbs 11:11**

~ They bring harm and devastation upon themselves. **Proverbs 11:17**

~ Those who trust in the material wealth they have created will tumble.
Proverbs 11:28

The bottom line is, there will be disastrous and irreversible consequences for those who ignore Wisdom.

Using a Wasgij Perception to See a Different Picture

Evildoers foster rebellion against God;
the messenger of death will be sent against them.

Proverbs 17:11

When we build a Wasgij puzzle, we create a picture we hadn't seen before. In a similar way, let's decipher what Wisdom can give us by inverting the proverbs 17:11 reading:

The wise and upright person encourages and cultivates collaboration with God, that Life will be with them and move for them.

Read those words slowly and drink in their beauty. Here is treasure beyond belief.

Time to reflect:

Which of these Proverbs triggers a warning signal for you?

What is that saying to you?

"The wise and upright person encourages and cultivates collaboration with God, that Life will be with them and move for them. "

Reflect on the words above. What does it mean to you that Life will be with you and move for you?

Notice how you feel as you reflect upon those words?

What does that mean about how you choose to live your life?

What difference could that make to your business and to your life?

As we wrap up, which of Wisdom's treasures have caught your attention?

Chapter 61

Treasures Beyond Belief

Seeking Wisdom is a life journey, rather than a final destination. At times, we will meander; we will forget the path we need to be on. Then we need to pause to decipher the clues that were hidden in plain sight. We need to slow down to see them and figure out Wisdom's message.

And sometimes we might take a tumble before we see what was before our eyes all the time.

In all your ways acknowledge Him
and he shall direct your paths.

Proverbs 3:6 NKJV

In the NIVUK version of this verse, "direct your paths" is translated as "make your paths straight". If the path is straight it is much easier to see what's ahead! Often, the path of business feels uneven - there are dips and turns on the journey. So, what might this verse mean?

I don't see God as a "fairy godmother" figure who waves a magic wand and *Ta-dah! Everything is transformed! The path is straight!* I perceive that God wants us to grow to our fullest potential. We wouldn't mature - we wouldn't be stretched - if God waved a magic wand whenever we hit challenges. So, does He "straighten the path"? Then it occurs to me - God looks at the "big picture" of life. If we were to view our life path from an aerial view, it could appear straight. Maybe - if we can stand back, look at the unfolding picture and imagine God's perspective - we would realise the path is straighter than it seems to us in the midst of our everyday twists and turns, ups and downs and deviations. We will see the way unfolding if we look at the big picture rather than worry about the bump or twist on the path.

Our life journey unfolds step by step, as we walk the adventure trail of Wisdom.

> *The upright will walk in the land,*
> *and the blameless will remain in it;*
>
> **Proverbs 2:21**

What does "land" symbolise?

~ A means of making a living

~ Security

~ Continuity

~ Peace

~ Grounded

~ Stability

~ Providing for our needs and those of others

~ Something that continues after us - a legacy.

How do we achieve this? By being upright and blameless in all we do. How do we achieve being upright and blameless? Solomon makes it clear - we need to seek Wisdom; *then* we'll discover riches beyond belief.

Discovering the Treasures of Wisdom

> *He who gets wisdom loves his own soul.*
>
> **Proverbs 19:8 NKJV**

Gaining Wisdom is about more than our physical existence. The one who seeks Wisdom knows that their spiritual well-being matters too.

When we follow Wisdom, here are some of the promises:

~ You won't get entangled in traps that could ruin you. **Proverbs 3:26b**

~ Your way will be safe. **Proverbs 3:23a**

~ Freedom. **Proverbs 11:21**

~ Understanding and foresight. **Proverbs 8:12**

~ Riches and honour. **Proverbs 3:16**

~ Favour and a good name (reputation) - with God and with people. **Proverbs 3:4**

~ Pleasantness and peace. **Proverbs 3:17**

~ Security. **Proverbs 18:10**

~ You won't be afraid of a sudden catastrophe overwhelming you. **Proverbs 3:25**

~ You will be able to sleep at night. **Proverbs 3:24**

~ Blessing – and the tree of life. **Proverbs 3:18**

~ The Lord will be the One you can rely upon. **Proverbs 3:26a**

~ God takes into his confidence those who chose to live by the code of Wisdom. **Proverbs 3:32**

What an awesome thought. God will share with us those things closest to His heart - those things that cause Him pain and joy; those things that He desires to see fulfilled, for His kingdom of peace, love and harmony to come to earth. **God will share with us what is on His heart!**

Wisdom is Walking with God

Wisdom is as integral to the character of God as Love. It's who He is! **Wisdom causes that, when we are in tune with God, that which we desire becomes a reality. Wisdom is always aligned with God's eternal values. The unimaginable becomes tangible.** The qualities of Wisdom are the qualities of God. It is this same Wisdom that created the entire universe.[114] Wisdom made life itself possible! The whole universe was imagined into being.

There is always a final code that Indiana has to crack to enter into the inner chamber, where unimaginable riches lie undiscovered. Indiana is able to decipher the clues because of his knowledge of ancient texts. Others have rushed in without observing or understanding the clues.

In Proverbs there is a key expression that is challenging to decipher. We repeatedly read the words the "fear of the LORD", but its mystery eludes us. We need the eyes of an adventuring archaeologist to understand. The translated word "fear" is too narrow. In our culture, "fear" implies an expectation of punishment. Yet Proverbs 2:5 says if we truly seek Wisdom we will "understand the fear of the LORD and find the knowledge of God." In our language, "fear" sounds a contradiction to being in relationship with a loving God who holds us in his confidence. So, what might be encoded in this phrase? What does "Fear of the LORD" mean? What secret chambers might it unlock? We need a sleuth's mindset to unlock the metaphor. I find an unexpected key in a different movie series: *The Chronicles of Narnia*. Mr Beaver's words, describing the great Lion Aslan, adored by the children, in *The Lion, the Witch and the Wardrobe* help me to understand. He exclaims that Aslan isn't *safe* - but he is *good!* He is the King!

Blessed is the one who always trembles before God,
Proverbs 28:14

Peoplespeak: If you truly seek Wisdom you will get to understand things so awesome that you'll quake in your boots. You'll discover things you had thought were beyond understanding.

The term "the fear of the LORD" isn't easy to comprehend. If I reword it, "When I gaze on the awesomeness of God" then I begin to understand.

The fear of the LORD leads to life;
Then one rests content, untouched by trouble.
Proverbs 19:23

I can gaze on the awesomeness of God; and be at peace.

That doesn't mean that trouble won't arise, but trouble won't overcome the hero. There would be no exciting story if there was no challenge. Like Indiana, our quest will be an adventure. It's Wisdom that will lead us to awesome success.

> *Those who trust in themselves are fools,*
> *but those who walk in wisdom are kept safe.*
>
> Proverbs 28:26

An adventure is a story of overcoming challenges, of heroic exploits and life-changing outcomes.

Will you take the challenge of stepping out into the most exciting adventure you can ever take? The adventure is never over! There is always more to discover.

Time to reflect:

What three "Wisdom" promises do you most desire in your life?

What might be blocking the abundance of these promises from flowing in your business and your life?

What would it mean in your life and business to know the awesomeness of God?

Chapter 62

The Discovery

In starting my entrepreneurial journey, my initial quest was to create a profitable business whilst making a difference in people's lives – but, like so many before me, the reality was challenging.

In my search for success, I have gained a different, healthier attitude towards wealth, and Proverbs has opened her treasure vault to reveal far greater riches.

I trust this book has inspired you **to transform your passion into profitability, live your life fully and make a difference in the world.** Wisdom's lessons are not just about us as individuals – each one of us is part of God's grand design. Whilst we want rules for life and rules for business, I perceive that love is the kernel in Solomon's teachings on Wisdom.

What is love? My favourite definition of love, apart from 1 Corinthians 13, is Scott Peck's frame of extending ourselves to cause the other person's growth.[115] What does love have to do with business? I believe that, as business leaders, we have the power to create a kinder, more compassionate and loving world.

When we start a business, so many of us focus on the dream of financial gain. My vision is that this book will inspire you to discover that your business can be so much more than a profit-making machine.

Wisdom can guide us to create transformative businesses - that help all of us as human-beings in community to grow towards our wonder-full God-given potential.

Blessings,

Val

P.S. I would love to hear how the thoughts in this book have impacted your life and your business.

Please connect with me on author@valmullally.com

If this book has been helpful to you, I would greatly appreciate it if you would please write a review on Amazon, or other online retailer where you bought this book, or on my social media platforms. This matters because potential readers are guided by feedback that others have given.

Want to dig deeper? In the appendices, I will show you the tools I used to peek inside Wisdom's treasure chest.

Appendix 1

How I Unearthed Treasure in Ancient Biblical Texts

I read the first chapter of Proverbs then stared at the page. *Hmmm. Nothing is jumping up and hitting me between the eyes. Will I gain anything significant from reading a chapter a day?*

I reread it more slowly, noticing verses that pertained to business.

What if I use a journal and write out any insights I gain?

The process of physically writing out the verses slowed me down, in that I engaged more deeply with the text. If I approached this as an adventure, with Indiana Jones' astute eyes, what might I discover? What were the hidden keys to business success?

Perhaps you want to take the challenge to set out on this adventure of discovery yourself. If you open a Bible to the centre pages you will find yourself in the book of Proverbs - right at the heart of God's message to humanity! I recommend using a Bible translation that gives the richness of language that enables you to dig for the deep meaning. Some versions of the Bible, such as the "Good News for Modern Man" which is a paraphrase, are easier to read but, in my opinion, the vocabulary is shallow. The language is deliberately simplified to make it easier to read. This means that the richness of the text has been 'dumbed down", and at times may not be fully accurate;

which means it loses, and at times distorts, some of the rich treasures of these writings. Please remember, I am not a trained theologian, nor an expert on translation or the culture of this geographic region, nor I am knowledgeable concerning this phase of history. This book is a record of my own naive exploration. I often prayed for God to give me insight – and was amazed how perspectives I had never seen before revealed themselves to me. I share my thoughts here – but, please, study the ancient scriptures for yourself. Find other books and commentaries about the book of Proverbs if you want to discover the jewels that I have missed.

Here is how I embarked on my journey. Please take what is useful to you. Each day I read and reread the chapter, and then contemplated how I was going to record what I was noticing. I decided not to use a Study Bible or Commentaries to expand my understanding in my first reading through the Proverbs. I would do that later, but I let my first reading be led by my own curiosity, trusting God to guide me.

Appendix 2
Tips for Exploring Ancient Biblical Texts

~ Write by hand.

This slows down the process, and you will notice things you didn't see before.

~ Read a chapter. Read again. Then assess what will help you to discover the gems.

On exploring different chapters I found I needed a different approach to help me see what was before me and to assimilate what I was discovering. In reading some chapters, I found it helpful to create a table noting the positive and negative characteristics and the outcomes of each. (See juxtapositions - below).

~ Ask yourself, "What does this word actually mean?"

I became aware of "old fashioned" words that I wouldn't normally use in my own speech. Words such as "prudent". What does that actually mean? I looked on the internet to check the meaning of words and to find synonyms. I wrote out these discoveries, and these often enlarged my thinking. Looking up the definition of words like "prudent" gave me insights into key principles of wisdom, especially as they pertained to business.

Check definitions, synonyms and antonyms of words to discover more complex and nuanced meanings.

~ Notice the position of this message in the overall layout of Proverbs and in the chapter.

Like newspapers, the messages early in the text indicate priority issues. What are the "headline" messages?

~ Ask yourself, "What is the theme of this passage?"

Look for repeated themes within different Proverbs. How are these themes enlarged upon? For example, record the different verses about the slacker. Compare these verses and journal what you notice.

~ Notice where themes/topics are repeated or expanded upon.

A repetition indicates that something is important. Some messages are repeated in other words immediately. Other messages are repeated later in the chapter or in later chapters, perhaps in different wording. e.g. Re: social justice in Proverbs 28:3 and also Proverbs 28:8

~ Observe juxtapositions. And create your own.

For example, Proverbs list the mindset, behaviours and the consequences of acting like a fool. What are the opposites? Use "negative" and "positive" columns to create your own juxtapositions.

In sections, such as Proverbs 17, only the negative aspect - "the fool" - is described. Ponder what the implied opposites might be.

~ Seek to understand the cultural context.

Think of the geography, the historical times and cultural context. What meaning unfolds? Sometimes, apparently simple phrases take on a deeper meaning and obscure passages reveal their treasures when you do this.

~ Unfold the metaphor.

When you notice an image or an unusual word, ask yourself what else that might mean.

The amazing thing is that neuroscience now recognises that the left hemisphere of the brain processes logic whilst the right hemisphere of the brain processes images. Meditate on the metaphors of the language to discover depths and nuances that could easily be missed, or not deeply understand. Proverbs is not mere a "to do" list. Seek out its treasures.

Here is an example:

> *Better to meet a bear robbed of her cubs*
> *than a fool bent on folly.*
>
> **Proverbs 17:12**

Think of it - a bear robbed of her cubs is in a totally reactive state. There is no reasoning with her. And she is capable of wreaking havoc. No one wants to be anywhere near a raging bear! Often the deepest message lies within the poetry. Solomon alludes to that in the opening verses of the Proverbs. These Wisdom writings are for "understanding proverbs and parables, the sayings and riddles of the wise." [116]

~ Consider what the modern equivalent to the lyrical language might be.

Proverbs refer to "kings" and "servants".

What understanding unfolds if we consider how these attributes can be applied to "leader/employer" and "team member/employee"?

What other words could be reconsidered to make the message more meaningful in our modern-day context?

~ Explore more deeply.

I tried to hold in mind, "What is the author's intent?"

"Who is this written for and why?"

I tried to "step back" and see the big picture. I considered the literary style. What was given priority in the overall structure? What was given priority in a section? Where does a new thought or a new expression first appear? Where was repetition or juxtaposition used for emphasis? And what was the possible significance of the beginning and ending verses in a section?

And, importantly, I checked the meaning of many of the "old fashioned" words that appeared in the text. Establishing the accurate meaning of words such as "prudent" and "fool" deepened my understanding.

Only after this first round of my own exploration of Proverbs did I begin to use Bible Study materials to dig deeper.

As you search the Scriptures, I pray you will find wealth beyond what you had ever imagined.

Be still and know that I am God.

Be still and know that I am.

Be still and know.

Be still.

Be.

Help Val to Help Other Entrepreneurs

Thank you for reading this book. If these chapters have given you helpful insights into how to create a successful business that is founded on the principles of Wisdom, then please help me to spread this message.

Please visit Amazon, or the online platform where you purchased this book, or Goodreads, to write a review. This matters because most potential readers first judge a book by what others have to say.

Please share the details of this book with anyone who you think will benefit from *Discovering the Secrets of Business Success in Ancient Biblical Wisdom*. If you mention this book on social media, please use the hashtag #BizWisdomBook

I greatly appreciate your support because you help others discover how we, as business leaders, have the power to create truly successful businesses, that create a kinder, more compassionate and loving world.

Thank you.

Val Mullally MA

Recommended Resources for Business Success

Relational Skills Online Courses by Val Mullally

For insights regarding how to integrate the relational skills discussed in this book into your work, sign up for an online course with Val. She combines her skills as an experienced educator together with her training and capability as a life-coach, supervisor, a community leader and authorpreneur to offer you a unique opportunity to train with her. Visit https://bit.ly/RelationalSkillsOnlineCourses to discover more.

Exclusive Masterclass Series for Organisation and Business Leaders, and Entrepreneurs

The wisdom of Proverbs is potentially transformative, and the invitation is to consistently put our new learning into practice, within the challenges of everyday life.

Join accredited coach Val Mullally in an exclusive online group of like-minded professionals. Here is your chance to change your passion into profitability, and make a difference in the world.

Click this link to discover more: https://valmullally.com

Additional Supports

EGBSoulpreneurs - putting soul back into business https://egbsoulpreneurs.ie

Smarter Egg - helping you develop your working wisdom https://smarteregg.com

Listening

Kline, Nancy (1999) *Time to Think – listening to ignite the human mind* Cassell Illustrated, London

Entrepreneurship

Allende, Sam Conniff (2018) *Be More Pirate – or how to take on the world and win* Penguin Random House, UK

Holiday, Ryan (2017) *Perennial Seller – The Art of Making and Selling Work that Lasts* Profile Books Ltd, London

Inspiration

Delosa, Jack *Unwritten: Reinvent Tomorrow* (audiobook)

https://www.jackdelosa.com/reinvent-tomorrow-an-insight-into-unwritten/

Values and Integrity

Demartini, John F. (2013) *The Values Factor: The Secrets to Creating and Inspiring a Fulfilling Life* The Berkley Publishing Group, New York

Payne, Ruby K. (2019) *A Framework for Understanding Poverty* aha! Process, Inc., Highland, Texas

Rohr, Richard (2011) *Falling Upwards: A Spirituality for the Two Halves of Life* John Wiley and Sons, Inc., London

Quinn, Robert E. (2004) *Building the Bridge As You Walk On It – a guide for leading change* Jossey-Bass, San Francisco

Productivity

Allen, David (2015) *Getting Things Done: The Art of Stress-free Productivity* Piatkus, London

Allcott, Graham (2014) *How to Be A Productivity Ninja – Worry Less, Achieve More, Love What You Do* Icon Books Limited, London

Goldsmith, Marshall (2016) *Triggers: sparking positive change and making it last* Profile Books, London

Bibliography

Holy Bible, New International Version® Anglicized, NIV® Copyright © 1979, 1984, 2011 by Biblica, Inc.®

Holy Bible, New King James Version®. Copyright © 1982 by Thomas Nelson.

Allcott, Graham (2014) *How to Be a Productivity Ninja – Worry Less, Achieve More, Love What You* Do Icon Books, London

Branson, Richard *Losing My Virginity* – Kindle edition

Draper, Derek (2018) Create Space – *How to Manage Time, and Find Focus, Productivity and Success* Profile Books, London

El, Nir with Hoover, Ryan (2019) Hooked – *How to Build Habit-Forming Products* Penguin, USA

Glaser, Judith (2014) *Conversational Intelligence – How Great Leaders Build Trust and Get Extraordinary Results* Bibliomotion, New York

Grahl, Tim (2018) *Running Down a Dream – Your Road Map to Winning Creative Battles* Black Irish Entertainment Ebook Edition

Lerner, Harriet Goldhor (1993) *Dance of Deception - pretending and truth-telling in women's lives* Harper Collins Publishers, New York

Lavine, Sage (2017) *Women Rocking Business; the ultimate step-by-step guidebook to create a thriving life doing the work you love* Hay House Inc., United States

Lewis, C.S. (1950) *The Chronicles of Narnia - The Lion, the Witch and the Wardrobe* HarperCollins Children's Books, London

Maurya, Ash (2016) *Scaling Lean - Mastering the Key Metrics for Startup Growth,* Penguin, Random House, UK

McKeown, Greg (2014) *Essentialism - The Disciplined Pursuit of Less* Random House, Croydon, UK

Navarro, Joe (2008) *What Every Body Is Saying: An Ex-FBI Agent's Guide to Speed Reading People* Collins Publishers, New York

Newberg, Andrew MD and Waldman, Mark Robert (2009) *How God Changes Your Brain - Breakthrough Findings from a Leading Neuroscientist* Ballantine Books, New York

Peck, Scott (1978) *The Road Less Travelled* Arrow Books, London

Senge, Peter; Scharfer, C. Otto; Jaworski, Joseph and Flowers, Betty Sue (2004) *Presence - exploring profound change in people, organisations and society* Nicholas Brealy Publishing, London

Settle, Ben (2012 -2016) *Christian Business Secrets - how to use ancient laws to build a thriving godly business in today's cut-throat marketplace* Ben Settle

Siegel, Daniel J. ((2007) *The Mindful Brain - Reflection and Attunement in the Cultivation of Well-Being* W.W. Norton and Company, London

Silk, Danny (2009) *Culture Of Honour - Sustaining a Supernatural Environment* Destiny Image Publishers Inc., USA

Sincero, Jen (2017) *You Are a Badass at Making Money: Master the Mindset of Wealth* John Murray Learning, London

Sinek, Simon (2009) *Start With Why: How Great Leaders Inspire Everyone to Take Action*, Penguin Books, London

Other Books by Val Mullally

Helpful Resources for Wise Parenting

Mullally, Val (2020) *BEHAVE - What to Do When Your Child Won't* Orla Kelly Publishing, Ireland

Mullally, Val (2018) *Baby and Toddler On Board* Orla Kelly Publishing, Ireland

Mullally, Val (2018) *Stop Yelling – 9 Steps to Calmer, Happier Parenting* Orla Kelly Publishing, Ireland

For details see https://bit.ly/ValsBooks2Read

Acknowledgements

This book would never have been born without the input of many different people.

Firstly, my acknowledgement to the divine source, whom I know as God, whose Spirit has inspired this book.

To my father, no longer in this world, and to my dear mother: thank you for raising us in a home where the Bible was core to our way of being in this world.

To my husband Bill – without your support in so very many ways, I might not have realised my dream to become an author.

My heartfelt appreciation to all who have supported in so many roles, especially editor Ruth Ann Dell and proof-reader Claire Latinis Forde, who have given so many hours of their wisdom and guidance.

Thank you to talented cover designer Les German for the inspiring cover, and also to artist Rev. John Bower and graphic designer JK Shutt for the sensitive illustration of the Tree of Wisdom. The art work captures the essence of this book.

Special thanks to Aodan Enright of Smarter Egg, Ireland **smarteregg.com** who has generously written the Foreword, which sets the tone of this book, and to ever-patient Orla Kelly **orlakellypublishing.com** for her guidance, encouragement and professional publishing expertise.

My appreciation to all who have given suggestions and feedback, with particular thanks to Elizabeth Garry Brosnan of EGBSoulpreneurs **egbsoulpreneurs.ie** and Tanja Jensen Mullally for their wise feedback. I greatly appreciate the support of Project Coach Patricia Tiernan of Leap Coaching, Ireland, **leapcoaching.ie** for her commitment to helping me keep the book's progress on track.

Thanks also to Rebecca Mahon of Savvy Business Gals **savvybusinessgals.com** for her belief in my work and for all her helpful business advice and encouragement.

Thanks also to talented and patient webmaster Gabriel Merovingi **merovingi. com** whose guidance and support regarding all things relating to providing a website is invaluable.

To those with whom I have worked alongside, including those whose fleeting encounter left an impression, I thank you.

My appreciation for all the people whom I may never meet, whose work has supported this book's writing, production and distribution.

To all who have encouraged me, especially in the moments I doubted, you know who you are – blessings and deep appreciation. My apologies to those whom I have not named, who have helped along the journey of this book's writing and publishing.

To all whose shoulders I have stood upon - authors, mentors, trainers, lecturers - you gave me a greater and a wider vision, thank you.

I also acknowledge everyone who reads and supports my work. You make it possible for me to continue to create new resources. Together we are creating a wiser, more compassionate world.

* * *

Endnotes

1 Branson,Richard *Losing My Virginity* Kindle location 6706

2 Branson,Richard *Losing My Virginity* Kindle location 1285

3 Settle 2012:182. Also, interviewee Ryan Healy shares that he seeks Wisdom in the book of Proverbs.

4 2 Chronicles 1:1-10

5 1 Kings 3:9

6 2 Chronicles 1:11-12

7 Proverbs 1:10-33 NIV

8 https://dictionary.cambridge.org/dictionary/english/complacency 9/10/19

9 Proverbs 2:1-22

10 Proverbs 3:2,9,16, 17

11 Proverbs 3:6

12 Proverbs 3:8

13 Proverbs 3:16

14 Proverbs 3:17

15 Proverbs 3: 17

16 Proverbs 1:1-7

17 https://www.lexico.com/en/definition/prudent 8/11/19

18 Latin vocationem; a calling /a being called. https://www.etymonline.com/word/vocation 9/10/2019

19 *Centre for Action and Contemplation* email 21/3/19

20 Proverbs 3 NIV

21 https://www.dictionary.com/browse/discern 9/12/19

22 For more re how our brain is connected to our gut see Glaser 2014, 3-6

23 For a mail system that works, see the "Email" chapter in *Productivity Ninja* by Graham Allcott.

24 https://en.wikiquote.org/wiki/Greg_McKeown_(author) 17/9/19

25 One of the key insights I gained from being part of a Smarter Egg Peer Circle in Cork, Ireland with Aodan Enright. See https://smarteregg.com/what-we-do/

26 https://lifehacker.com/how-long-it-takes-to-get-back-on-track-after-a-distract-1720708353 14/10/19

27 Maurya 2016:22-23

28 https://rsc.byu.edu/archived/christopher-columbus-latter-day-saint-perspective/first-voyage-americas-columbus-guided 4/2/19

29 "Simple" refers to those who are gullible. https://www.biblica.com/bible/niv/proverbs/1/ 7/5/19

30 Footnote 'a' on https://www.biblica.com/bible/niv/proverbs/1/ 2/10/19

31 Holiday 2017:55

32 *Hooked* by Nir Eyal 2019:1 quoting I*DC-Facebook Always Connected.pdf*

33 https://ancient-hebrew.org/definition/sin.htm 05/02/20

34 Proverbs 1:8-19

35 Proverbs 7:27

36 Silk, 2009:128-145

37 https://www.psychologytoday.com/us/blog/turning-straw-gold/201408/20-quotations-generosity-profound-act-kindness 18/10/19

38 Judges 20:16

39 See also Proverbs 19:29

40 Lavine 2017, chapter 12

41 https://www.sciencedaily.com/releases/1997/12/971227000141.htm 15/10/19

42 See also Proverbs 10:14

43 Proverbs 1:10

44 http://www.leaderu.com/orgs/probe/docs/char-def.html 16/11/19

45   https://www.lexico.com/en/definition/complacency 14/10/19

46   English Standard Version

47   Check out Proverbs 6:6-11, 19:15, 20:13, 23:21, 24:30-34 regarding other sluggardly habits.

48   See Lavine 2017 chapter 3 for more re taking action to create clarity.

49   https://rsc.byu.edu/archived/christopher-columbus-latter-day-saint-perspective/first-voyage-americas-columbus-guided 4/2/19

50   https://www.jackdelosa.com/reinvent-tomorrow-an-insight-into-unwritten/ 16/11/19

51   Mullally, 2020 See final section of chapter eight.

52   Glaser 2014: xiii

53   O'Malley, Mary *What's in the way IS the way: The Transforming Power of Trusting Your Life – All of it*

54   Proverbs 8:13b

55   Proverbs 30:13

56   Proverbs 6:17

57   Proverbs 18:2

58   Proverbs 18:3

59   Newberg and Waldman, 2009:13

60   Newberg and Waldman, 2009:13

61   Proverbs 8:13b

62   https://www.encyclopedia.com/humanities/dictionaries-thesauruses-pictures-and-press-releases/plunder-1 8/11/2019

63   https://dictionary.cambridge.org/dictionary/english/plunder 13/3/19

64   Proverbs 3:17

65   *Centre for Action and Contemplation* Email 3/4/16

66   I mis-typed "Romans" 8:31 instead of "Proverbs". I invite you to look up this verse in the Bible to see the significance.

67   Quoted by Derek Draper in *Create Space - How to Manage Time, and Find Focus, Productivity and Success*

68 Proverbs 10:26

69 Further warnings against adultery in Proverbs 6 and 7.

70 https://en.wikipedia.org/wiki/Theory_of_multiple_intelligences

71 http://www.emotionalintelligencecourse.com/history-of-eq/

72 For more on this read Judith E. Glaser's book *Conversational Intelligence: How Great Leaders Build Trust and Get Extraordinary Results*

73 http://www.richardchuseman.com

74 https://www.lexico.com/en/definition/perverse 24/11/19

75 https://www.lexico.com/en/definition/undoing 7/10/19

76 https://www.wordhippo.com/what-is/the-opposite-of/undoing.html 7/10/19

77 See also Proverbs 26:22

78 https://www.lexico.com/en/definition/perverse 6/10/19

79 https://www.wordhippo.com/what-is/the-opposite-of/annoyed.html 3/06/19

80 https://www.biblegateway.com/passage/?search=Proverbs+25%3A11&version=GNT 7/12/19

81 https://www.lexico.com/en/definition/folly 6/10/19

82 Glaser 2014, 64

83 Peck1978/1992, 85

84 Proverbs 10:11 AMPC Amplified Bible, Classic Edition

85 Glaser 2014, xiii

86 Siegel 2007, 121f

87 https://www.scienceofpeople.com/microexpressions/ 8/10/19

88 https://www.goodreads.com/quotes/717-be-patient-toward-all-that-is-unsolved-in-your-heart 9/7/19

89 See also Proverbs 23:25, 27:11; 28:7, 24

90 Draper 2018, 141

91 Branson, Richard *Losing My Virginity* Kindle location 6560

92 See also Proverbs 28:23

93 Proverbs 19:4-7

94 Proverbs 28:7

95 Proverbs 3:21b

96 Proverbs 24:30

97 https://havingmycake.net/lerner3/ 8/10/19

98 https://www.bibleref.com/Proverbs/2/Proverbs-2-2.html 4/3/19

99 https://www.tandfonline.com/doi/abs/10.1080/00332927608410385?journal Code=upyp20
4/3/2019

100 https://www.lexico.com/en/definition/prudent 8/10/19

101 https://quoteinvestigator.com/2013/04/23/good-idea/ 05/02/20

102 Proverbs 31:8.9

103 https://www.brainyquote.com/quotes/robert_kennedy_745955 8/10/19

104 https://www.jfklibrary.org/archives/other-resources/john-f-kennedy-speeches/
inaugural-address-19610120 26/11/19

105 Draper 2018, 150

106 See also Proverbs 20:2

107 https://peacealliance.org/tools-education/peace-inspirational-quotes/
26/11/19

108 https://www.mentalfloss.com/article/63892/15-heroic-facts-about-florence-
nightingale 26/11/19

109 https://www.merriam-webster.com/dictionary/righteous 4/2/19

110 https://www.independent.co.uk/arts-entertainment/films/news/five-
surprising-truths-from-the-indiana-jones-films-a6948216.html 4/7/19

111 Proverbs 4:5

112 Proverbs 4:20-27

113 Proverbs 4:22

114 Proverbs 3:19 and Proverbs 19:20

115 Peck 1978/199:85

116 Proverbs 1:6 NIV

Printed in Poland
by Amazon Fulfillment
Poland Sp. z o.o., Wrocław